THREE VIEWS OF OMAN

WILFRED **THESIGER**

CHARLES **BUTT**

EDWARD **GRAZDA**

THREE VIEWS OF OMAN

WILFRED **THESIGER** CHARLES **BUTT** EDWARD **GRAZDA**

SOCIETY AND RELIGION 1945–2006

EDITED BY

RAINA SACKS **BLANKENHORN**

WITH A FOREWORD BY

SHEIKH ABDULLAH BIN **MOHAMMED AL-SALIMI**

Broadway Publications,

1841 Broadway, Suite 211,

New York NY 10023

First Edition 2012
Design: Alma Phipps & Associates
Printed in China

Three views of Oman: Wilfred Thesiger, Charles Butt, Edward
Grazda : society and religion 1945–2006 / edited by Raina Sacks
Blankenhorn ; with a foreword by Sheikh Abdullah al-Salimi. —
New York, NY : Broadway Publications, 2012.
p. ; cm.
ISBN: 978-1-931764-27-8 (hardbound) ; 978-1-931764-29-2 (paperback)

Includes bibliographical references.
Contains an essay entitled "A place one has never been",
by the editor, Raina Sacks Blankenhorn.

1. Oman—Pictorial Works. 2. Oman—Description and Travel.
3. Oman—Social Life and Customs—Pictorial Works. I. Blankenhorn,
Raina Sacks. II. Thesiger, Wilfred, 1910–2003. III. Butt, Charles,
1935–2006. IV. Grazda, Edward, 1947–. V. Three views of Oman: society
and religion 1945–2006. VI. A place one has never been.

DS247.O64 T47 2012
953/.53— dc23   1204

TABLE OF CONTENTS

ACKNOWLEDGMENTS

HE ARTISTIC WORK PRESENTED here comes from three distinguished photographic collections: the Wilfred Thesiger Collection at the Pitt Rivers Museum and the Charles Butt Collection at the Middle East Centre Archive of St. Antony's College, both at Oxford University, and the Edward Grazda Collection, at the Institute for American Values and at the Ministry of Awqaf and Religious Affairs, in Muscat. Creating this book was an ambitious effort that brought together important British, American, and Omani institutions across continents, time zones, and cultures. *Three Views of Oman: Society and Religion 1945–2006* celebrates not only the work of these outstanding photographers but also the partnership between the Ministry of Religious Affairs, the Middle East Centre, and the Institute for American Values that brought it to fruition.

I am most grateful to Sheikh Abdullah bin Mohammed al-Salimi, the minister of Awqaf and Religious Affairs, for his generosity, guidance, and support. I am also grateful to the board of directors of the Institute for American Values. Scholars Abdulrahman al-Salimi, the editor-in-chief of *Al-Tasamoh,* a research journal on contemporary issues in Islam, and Eugene Rogan, the director of the Middle East Centre at St. Antony's, shared their invaluable expertise to ensure the integrity of the project. Without the exuberant vision of Margaret MacMillan, the warden of St. Antony's College, who saw to it that publication would coincide with an exhibition of the works in these pages at St. Antony's College, none of this would have been possible. I am also grateful to Edward Grazda for his commitment to excellence and dedication to this project since its inception in 2005.

Additionally, I especially want to thank Mike O'Hanlon, the director of the Pitt Rivers Museum, and Christopher Morton, the museum's curator of photography and the acclaimed author of *Wilfred Thesiger in Africa,* for making Thesiger's works available; and Debbie Usher, the archivist at St. Antony's Middle East Centre, for her meticulous attention to detail and unfailing support. I appreciate too the numerous contributions of all our colleagues at the Institute for American Values and the Ministry of Religious Affairs; and my great friends Diana Parker and John Landers, who freely lent their advice and encouragement.

I am indebted to the following people for their gifts of friendship and talent in the creation of *Three Views of Oman:* Alma Phipps, Thomas Jockin, Clementine Hobson, Adam Berry, Alison Humes, Hassan Mneimneh, Ridwan al-Sayyed, David Blankenhorn, Barbara Whitehead, Charity Navarette, Doug Schneider, Jody Wood, Rachel George, Chuck Stetson, Allan Taylor, Peter Robinson, Pennie Cooke, and Joann Rasmussen. Thank you all.

—*Raina Sacks Blankenhorn*

A HISTORY IN PICTURES

OMAN, LIKE OTHER ARAB AND ISLAMIC societies, is the focus of widespread interest today. Yet the publication of *Three Views of Oman,* and its sister exhibition at St. Antony's College at Oxford University, is nearly the first portrait of the nation that highlights through its collection of photographs the evolving Omani relationship between religion and society, tradition and modernity.

This volume covers the past sixty-five years of our nation's history, from the end of the Second World War through the first decade of the twenty-first century. The photographs deal with subjects that are both sensitive and significant in Omani and Arabian society, namely, those variable and invariable elements of society that are inspired by faith and cultural values. The era covered by the pictures is one in which traditional values and customs have combined with the modern reality of Oman today, as it has been envisioned and planned by the policies of His Majesty Sultan Qaboos bin Said. A genuine knowledge of this period is vital for those wishing to influence future outcomes in the region.

The photographers Wilfred Thesiger, Charles Butt, and Edward Grazda show this complex aspect of Omani society with artistic creativity, sensitivity, and personal knowledge of and empathy for the Arabs, the East, and Oriental culture. Each in his own way is familiar with the historical and ethnographic issues implicit in the images and has a sincere commitment to the study of Eastern peoples and civilizations.

I hope that this exhibition will prove useful to scholars and artists as well as provide a valuable resource for researchers and students. It is vital that this material be presented in both Arab and Western cultural institutions.

Three Views of Oman and the exhibition at St. Antony's College denote for us in Oman the special significance of Britain's relationship with Africa and Asia in modern times and of academia's engagement with our societies and cultures.

My thanks go to everyone who has contributed to this project.

—*Sheikh Abdullah bin Mohammed al-Salimi*

A PLACE ONE HAS NEVER BEEN

OW DOES ONE UNDERSTAND a place one has never been? Or a person embedded in a history so thoroughly separate from one's own? The answer begins by listening to the other, recognizing what is universal and human, and ultimately, allowing for the possibility that there are some mysteries one does not understand. Looking at photographs—to see what is there and to ask what is not there—is a distinct way to experience the paradox of knowing and not knowing the other. The act itself is a step toward the engagement of one culture with another. Ours is a time of critical engagement between Western and Islamic cultures. Extremists on all sides have attempted to destroy what we have in common, to make monsters out of the other. Photographs can help counteract such characterizations by presenting an opportunity to take the time—lots of it—to look at images of the other in a subtle and reflective way. Then, when we take the time to look, all the disciplines slowly come into play: art history, architecture, history, anthropology, economics, technology, psychology—to name just some of the fields of knowledge we rely on to help us understand what we see when we look at a photograph.

Cultural critics of every sort, from formal classicists who focus on the plastic image to historical analysts who see the images as ideological texts, have prosecuted photography for its voyeurism. But we are absolutely aware, in this era of excruciating self-examination, of the prejudices of the culture, the photographer, the camera, the film, the subject, the setting. Everything is subjective, all are movable parts. That's what makes looking at images interesting and why we want to look—to find the secrets in the photographs and our perspective on them.

Photography is a silent medium. Perhaps that silence is what contributes to the pleasure of viewing a compelling image: The eyes look while the sensibilities are engaged, and the mind is free to wander. It is this openness, the ability to question what one sees, to work at understanding, to leave some things unsaid, or even unknown, that makes photography unique. Not everything can be defined: The viewer who takes this moment sees too that one culture does not know everything about another. We see what we know, what we can recognize as universal, as well as what makes us different. In this way we define ourselves as individuals and as individuals in a relationship of one culture to another.

Three Views of Oman, a collection of photographs taken by the explorer Wilfred

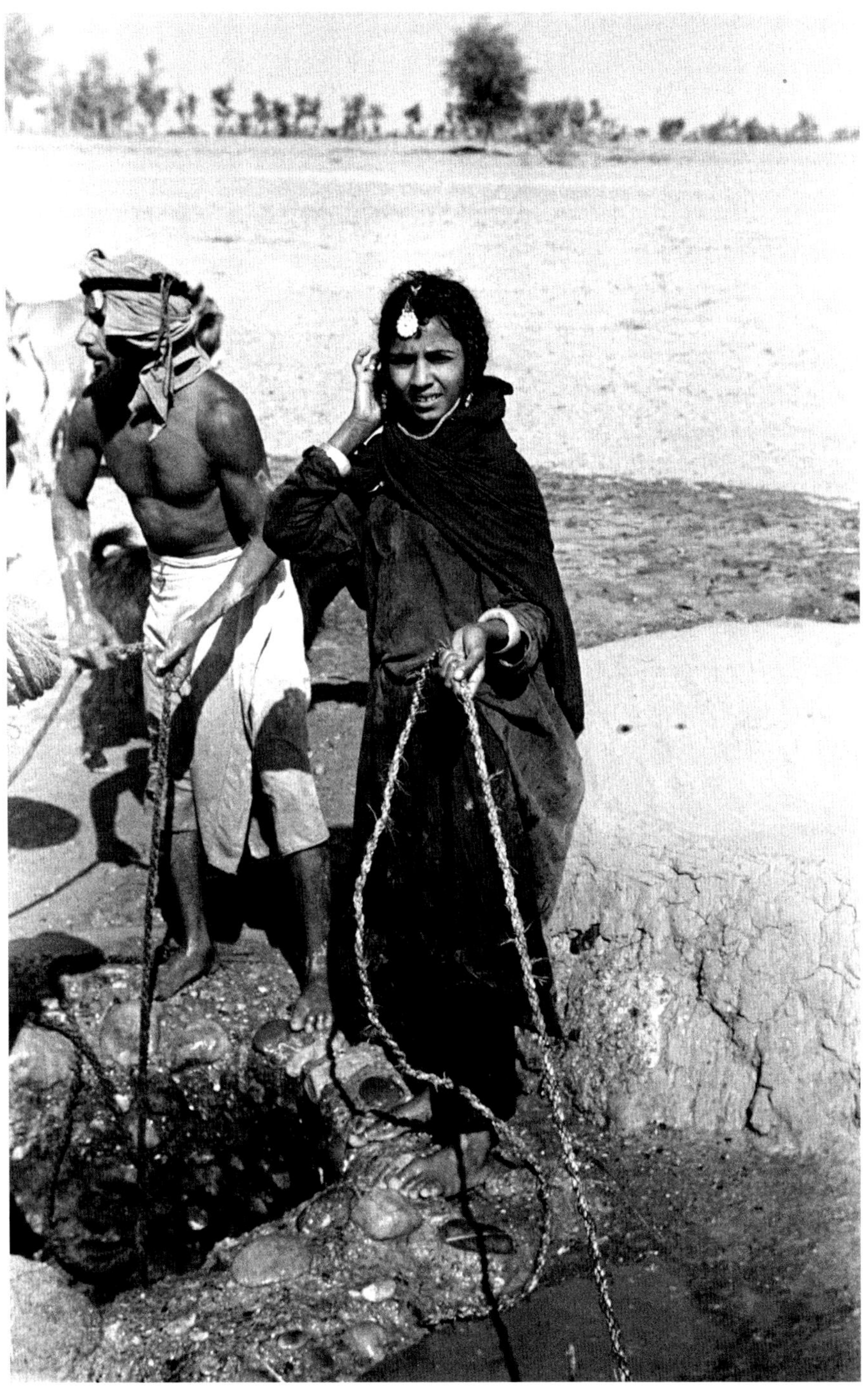

Fig. 1

Thesiger, the soldier Charles Butt, and the artist Edward Grazda, shows how each of these photographers views the world from an entirely different perspective, shaped by his own culture and his own distinctive moment in time. This book makes it easy to see that people do not perceive things in the same way, even when they are from the same culture, like Thesiger and Butt, both of whom are English. Even if one broadly uses the phrase Anglo-American to refer to the culture of the West, the three photographers as a group continue to be defined largely by their differences, underscoring the point that when we reach out to engage with other cultures we do so as individuals, grounded in our own highly developed particularity.

Thesiger was an experienced British officer when he arrived in 1945 on a mission for the Middle East Anti-Locust Unit. He crossed the Rub al-Khali (the Empty Quarter) at a time when the boundaries between Oman, Yemen, Saudi Arabia, and the Emirates were ill-defined. The desert was a dangerous place then: The Dhofar region in the south was engaged in a long-standing conflict with the sultanate, which by the 1950s turned into in a full-scale rebellion. This conflict intensified the historic struggle for power between the sultanate and the imamate. As oil was discovered in the desert, the region was further drawn into the politics of the Cold War, with England and the U.S. supporting the sultanate, and the Soviet Union supporting the rebels in Dhofar.

Thesiger was eager to travel across this violent and harsh terrain. During these arduous trips, he took intimate portraits of the people, mostly men, with whom he traveled. We see in these photographs that Thesiger knew his Bedouin companions well, some of whom became lifelong friends. The subjects look into the camera unafraid to gaze directly into Thesiger's eyes. A young woman of the Wahiba, her dignity and self-confidence apparent, is unperturbed by Thesiger's frank interest in her (fig. 1, and page 33). Thesiger could not resist taking her picture, one of a series of this woman, even though her examination of him suggests that they were not known to each other. What holds our attention and remains captivating seventy years later is the intimacy of these images, the subjects' ease with being photographed. Thesiger does not take images of what is ugly in life, which certainly doesn't mean that there wasn't ugliness to be seen, either in the life or in the people. But he doesn't want to be a part of it, so we see beauty. His eye for beauty and sensuality, his way of seeing, brings forward the folds of fabric, the color of skin, the light on the desert, the tactile and visceral nature of life (fig. 2, and page 25).

His image of the frankincense tree (page 13) is at first glance a spindly desert
tree. What holds Thesiger's attention or ours? The tree is a symbol and a reminder
that Oman's coastal cities have always played an important role in international trade.
The golden resin, produced only in this region and recognized in the West as a gift
offered to the baby Jesus, was for five thousand years a commodity linking Oman to
the east coast of Africa and Zanzibar, across the Arabian Sea to India, and north to
the ports of the Mediterranean. Thesiger knew, as we may not know when we look at
this austere image, that this tree has an enduring hold on history.

We also see these images as capturing time and creating memory. Not many people
took pictures in the desert in the 1940s and few who lived there remain to tell their
stories. Today desert resorts for tourists are appearing. There are roads and highways.
Some Omanis now humorously refer to the Empty Quarter as the Financial Quarter,
as the desert produces more than a million barrels of oil per day. So here is a record
of a time that has passed. This sense of a time gone by evokes melancholy in some,
because the past can suggest something purer. Thesiger himself loathed modernization. Others reject that view: For them the past recalls difficult times, and it is the
challenge and excitement of the future that holds their attention. All the same, these
photographs contain the memories of a place, the history of the people who lived there.

Charles Butt arrived in Oman twenty years later, in 1966, as a member of the
British Army Intelligence Corps. He stayed through the height of the Dhofar Rebellion, and was present when Sultan Taimur was forced out by his son, Sultan Qaboos,
in 1970. These were astounding times. Modernization was under way, the oil business
was booming. Unlike the isolationist policies of his father, Sultan Qaboos's response
to his country's problems was to strengthen its culture and build its infrastructure,
roads, water systems, and houses. Butt was right beside the young sultan and was
able to take his portrait (page 57). Through Butt's eyes, we see Sultan Qaboos busy
at work with other leaders, racing from one meeting to another (page 41); we watch
as the country begins a transition from a place lost in time, largely unknown to the
world, to a modern state.

Butt shoots in color and he looks at life differently from Thesiger. He is in a jeep,
he is in the air, he is all over the country and he is looking for information. What
are people doing on the coast? In the countryside? He shoots everything because
everything is interesting to him. During his time in Oman, Butt took more than

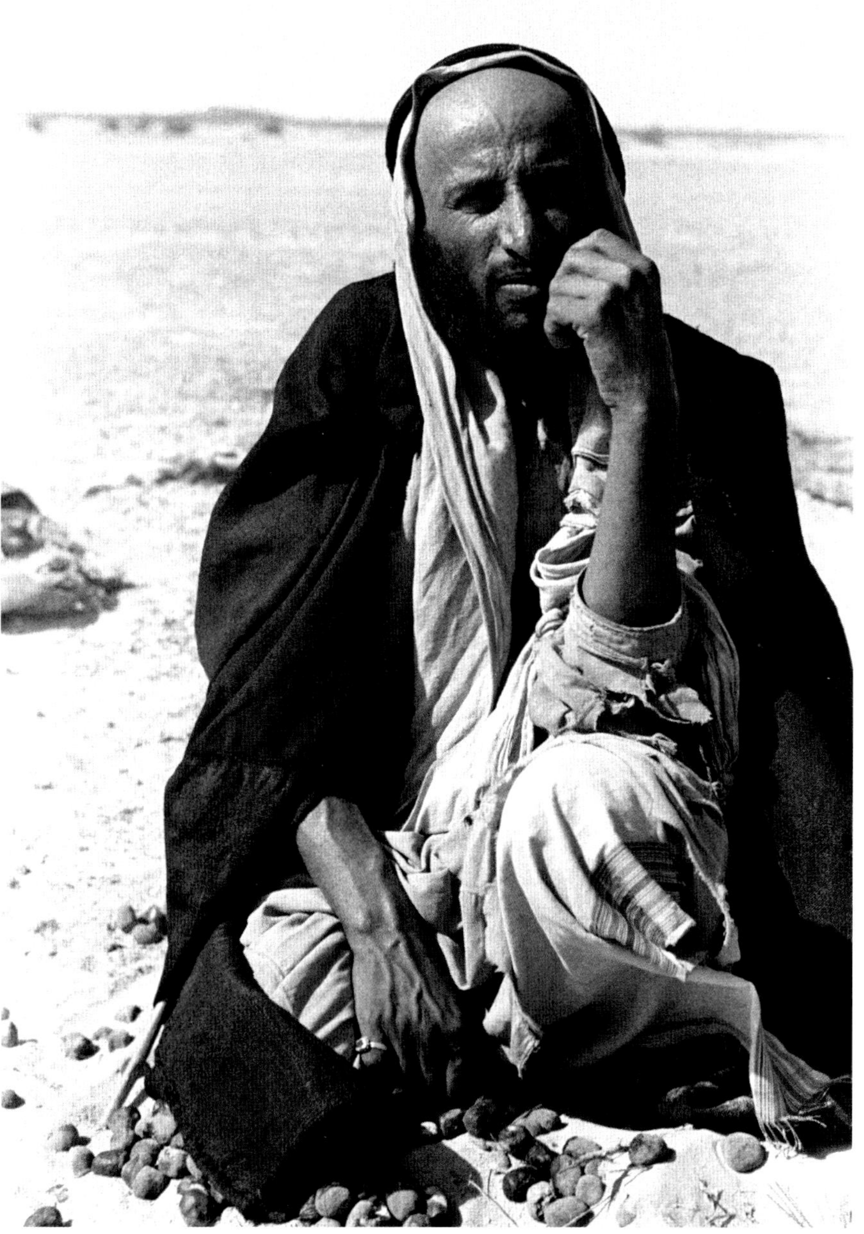

Fig. 2

seven thousand photographs. The intensity of the bright light reminds us of the heat. There is energy and dynamism to the narrative he sees taking place. He is interested in what's old, the ancient Ibadi cemetery (page 69), and what is new, the Shell sign announcing the presence of American oil companies (page 47). He is interested in children, men, women, celebrations, soldiers, those who are running the country and those who are not. People do not seem interested in him as he takes his pictures, nor is he interested in revealing himself to others. He's there, as the British are there, as part of the scenery, ubiquitous.

Notwithstanding that he was a soldier and an amateur photographer, his images are beautifully composed, bold, their color rich, reminding the viewer of the hot sun, the blue sky, and the intense hues of the Arabian Sea. This way of looking at the other is discreet because implicitly the distance between him and his subjects also describes the separation between their cultures. However, the dedication to taking this quantity of images and now having them preserved in an archive for scholars to use is a testament to Butt's passion both for photography and for this subject. These images add to the archive of visual culture of Oman and will be seen in the years ahead by scholars as a resource with which to understand what was taking place at this pivotal time in the country.

Unlike Thesiger and Butt, who spent years living in Oman, Edward Grazda arrived as a professional photographer on assignment for twelve weeks. Grazda is the quintessential outsider. He is not a part of a mission, neither an explorer like Thesiger nor a soldier like Butt. He is there on his own and he is alone. As an American he is at an even further remove from the culture than his predecessors, who had some advantage given the long-standing presence of Britain in the region. As a documentary photographer, Grazda is influenced by the photographers Robert Frank, who famously documented Americans in the 1950s, and Henri Cartier-Bresson, who sought in his images to capture the "decisive moment"—his description of the fraction of a second when the photographer, hardly observed by the subject, seizes life and catches it, as if beautifully art directed, on film. In his photographs of Oman, Grazda has created what critics recognize as iconic images. An Omani couple in the supermarket (fig. 3 and page 85), standing at rest, looks at the rows of goods available to them, but in opposite directions, seemingly hesitating to decide. This image suggests that the viewer is seeing the great challenge of modernization. But perhaps this is an idea we impose on the image. The angle of the view into the photo, from top down, suggests that these two people are standing close to each other; they could be husband and wife or they could be brother and sister, or they might be strangers. We do not know what they make of the objects of consumption around them, but we imagine that they are poised before a decision. The woman

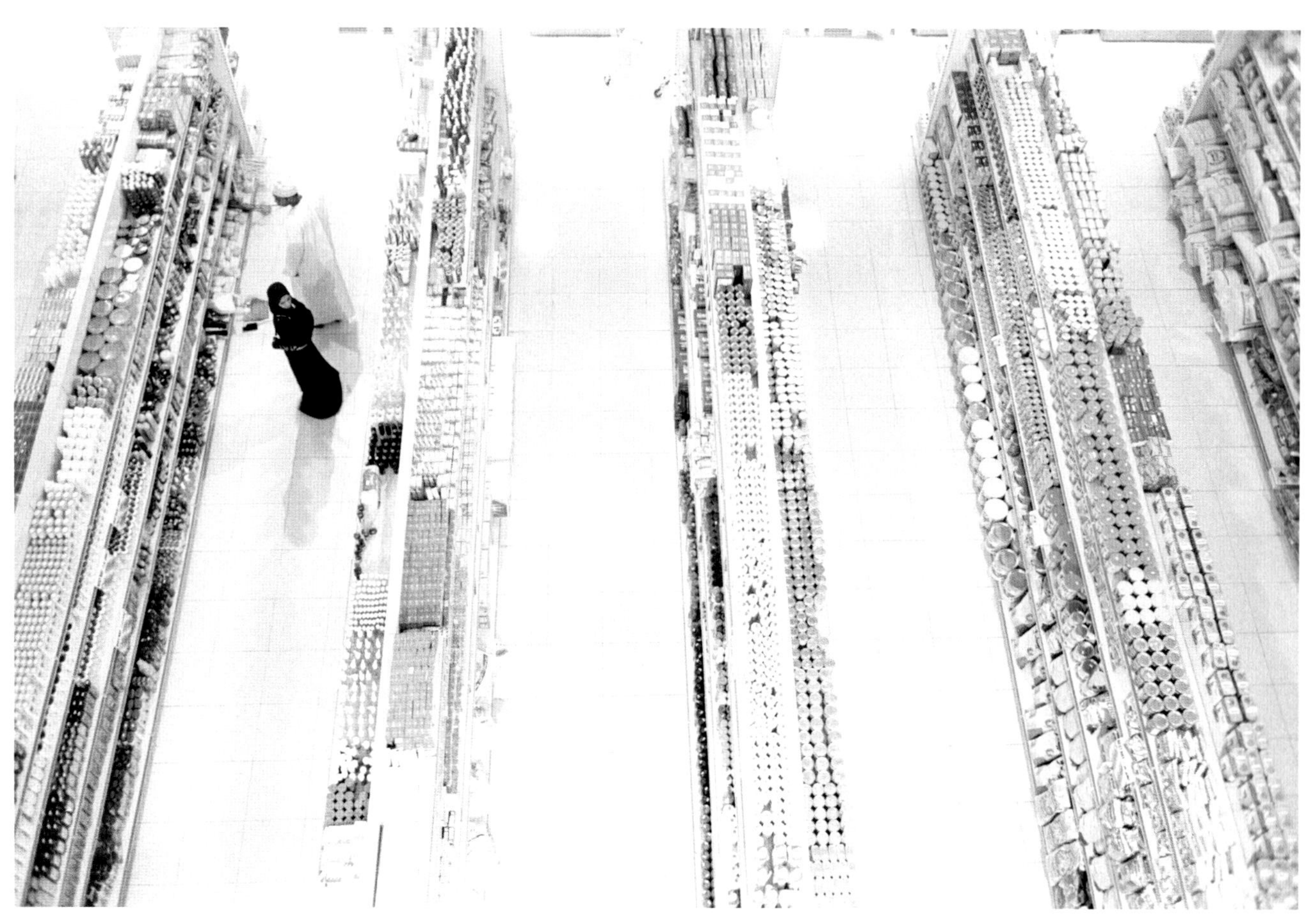

is wearing an abaya, a black robe that covers her slender body, along with a headscarf. We can see that she is young. We know very little else. The image is graphic, elegant to look at, mysterious. So it is a tableau upon which we are free to speculate.

In the image of three young boys on the Muttrah corniche taking Grazda's picture with their cell phones (fig. 4, and page 79), we see the humor and irony of the game "Are you looking at me? Because I am looking at you!" We see the boys, in traditional dress and with their phones, a mix of old and new, alongside a harbor with the sultan's yacht behind them. What do they see?

Grazda's photographs are not as emotional and tactile as Thesiger's, but both artists create objects of physical beauty. Grazda makes prints in which every detail is meticulously thought through—the choice of paper, the size of the image. The blacks are deep and rich. He is not interested in showing the world every image he took during his twelve-week visit. He is not interested in beauty per se as a subject.

He wants us to see what he has determined are good images. He looks at everything, including the ugly and the banal. A keen observer of peoples' habits, Grazda does not, like Butt, look at a subject head-on, but instead looks around and looks at an angle, at a man walking in front of a department store (page 107), or at a mother and child crossing a parking lot (page 89), at students on their way to school, at shoes left outside a door (page 102). He is interested in how people go about their daily lives, the small insignificant moments that slip by unnoticed unless the camera catches them.

Grazda arrived in 2006 to find gleaming five-star international hotels, and yet not one of his three thousand images is of tourists at the hotels or of international businessmen arriving for meetings, taking advantage of the security and beauty of the country to host conferences; nor are there images of crowded shopping centers or of the many couples walking alongside the beach at twilight. There are no grand visions of the landscape. He is not in the desert or in a plane or a jeep, but on foot. What interests him is seeing the choices people make, and how these precise moments captured on film reveal the social fabric of a culture.

In my role as curator, I chose these photographs over thousands of others, spending hours arguing with myself over why this one and not that one. In these choices, I have placed another sensibility, created another veil or an additional layer of perception for you, the viewer, to examine. The images hold secrets to the place and people of Oman, to its history, society, and religion, and to the intrepid photographers from England and America who peeked in and created this rich body of visual culture. *Three Views of Oman* is now a record of time and place, and in some small way helps us to grasp history.

—*Raina Sacks Blankenhorn*

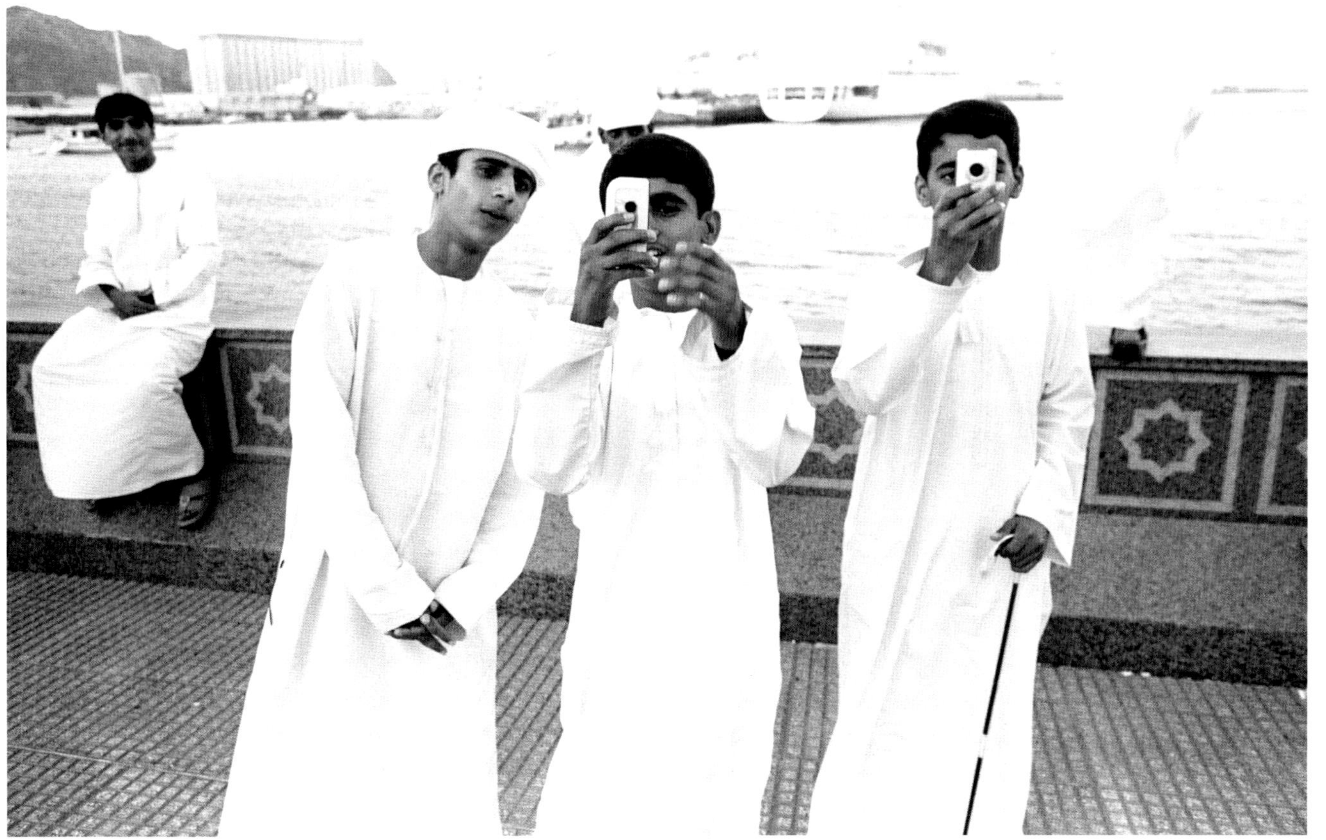

Fig. 4

IMPORTANT DATES IN THE HISTORY OF OMAN

1932 — Said bin Taimur, the Sultan of Muscat and Oman, accedes to the throne.

1955 — With the help of the British, Oman reestablishes control over the al-Buraimi oasis.

1957 — Oil is discovered in Oman.

1959 — The Jabal Akhdar war ends.

1970 — His Majesty Sultan Qaboos bin Said, eighth sultan of the al-Busaidi dynasty, accedes to the throne and declares the country unified as the Sultanate of Oman.

1970 — Introduction of the new Omani flag

1971 — Oman joins the United Nations.

1973 — Beginning of the performance of Friday prayers all over Oman

1975 — Demarcation of the maritime border with Iran

1976 — The Dhofar war ends.

1979 — Recognition of the Camp David peace accords

1981 — Establishment of the State Consultative Council

1985 — Formation of the Omani Royal Symphony Orchestra

1986 — Sultan Qaboos University, a public university of arts, science, and technology, opens in Muscat.

1990 — Demarcation of the border with Saudi Arabia

1991 — The Consultative Assembly (Majlis al-Shura) replaces the State Consultative Council.

1992 — Demarcation of the border with Yemen

1996 — The formulation and adoption of the Basic Law of the State, the Omani constitution

2001 — Sultan Qaboos Grand Mosque opens in Muscat. Demarcation of the border with UAE

2010 — Celebration of the nation's fortieth anniversary

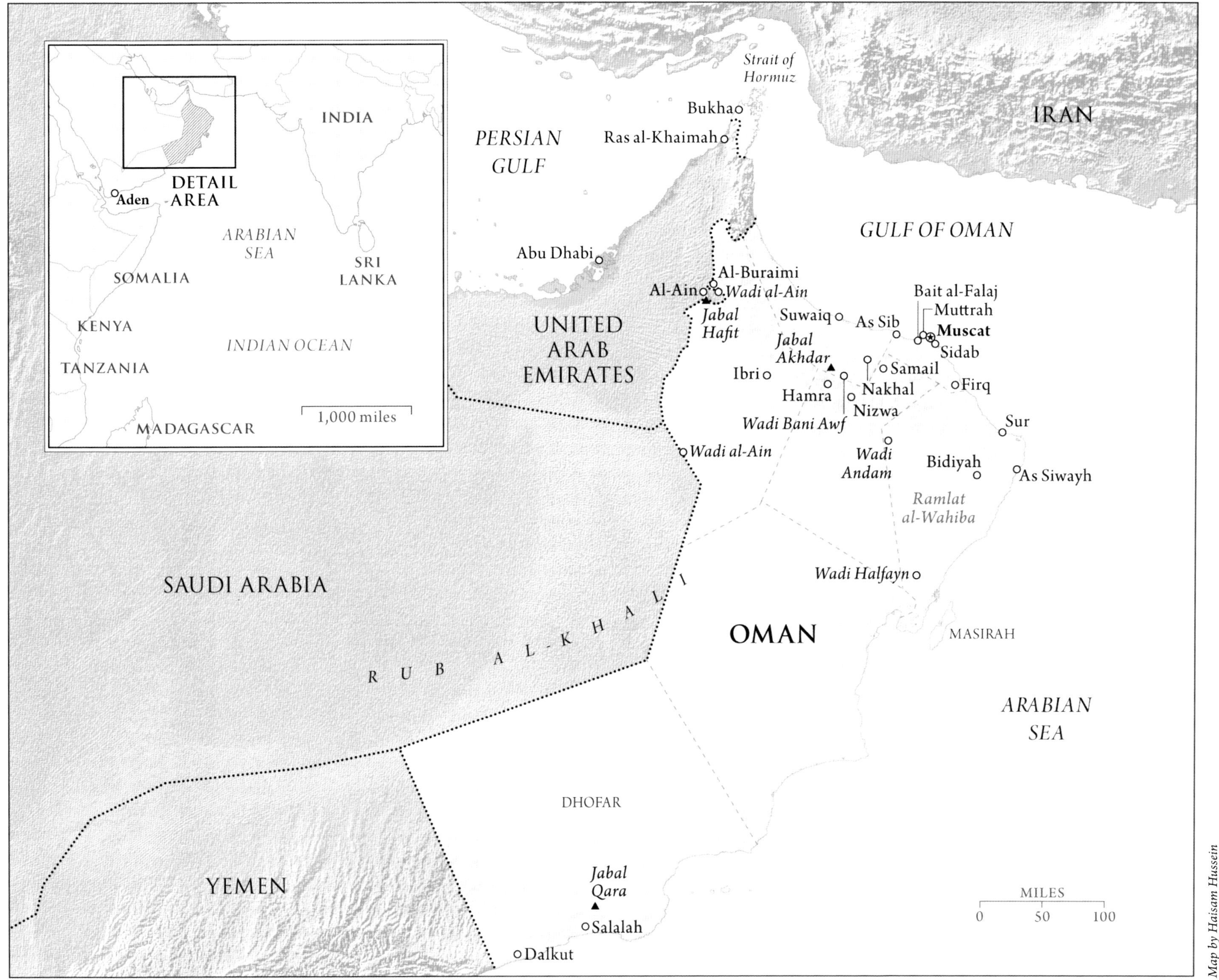
Strait of Hormuz
PERSIAN GULF
IRAN
Bukha
Ras al-Khaimah
GULF OF OMAN
Abu Dhabi
Al-Buraimi
Al-Ain
Wadi al-Ain
Jabal Hafit
Bait al-Falaj
Muttrah
Suwaiq
As Sib
Muscat
UNITED ARAB EMIRATES
Jabal Akhdar
Sidab
Ibri
Samail
Hamra
Nakhal
Firq
Nizwa
Wadi Bani Awf
Sur
Wadi Andam
Bidiyah
As Siwayh
Wadi al-Ain
Ramlat al-Wahiba
SAUDI ARABIA
Wadi Halfayn
OMAN
MASIRAH
R U B   A L - K H A L I
ARABIAN SEA
DHOFAR
Jabal Qara
YEMEN
Salalah
Dalkut
MILES
0   50   100

DETAIL AREA
INDIA
Aden
ARABIAN SEA
SRI LANKA
SOMALIA
KENYA
INDIAN OCEAN
TANZANIA
MADAGASCAR
1,000 miles

WILFRED THESIGER (1910–2003)

ORN IN ADDIS ABABA in 1910, Wilfred Patrick Thesiger spent his childhood in Abyssinia (now Ethiopia), where his father was the consul-general and minister plenipotentiary in charge of the British Legation. Reflecting later on his life, Thesiger wrote, "I am certain that the first nine years of my life have influenced everything that followed." Returning to England in 1919, to be educated at Eton College and Oxford University, and feeling out of place, Thesiger wanted to return to Africa. When in 1930 he received an invitation to Ras Tafari's coronation as Emperor Haile Selassie, he was eager to go. Thesiger's life of adventure began in earnest as this occasion gave him the opportunity to hunt and explore the country of his birth. He chose to follow the Awash River to its end—the last geographical puzzle in Abyssinia—providing him the chance to make his name as a traveler and explorer.

Thesiger's early photographs from the Awash River expedition were taken with a banged-up old box camera that had belonged to his father. Over time, he became more serious about his photography, as a record of his travels and to illustrate his published texts. After the Kodak box camera, Thesiger used four 35 mm Leicas: a Leica II from 1933 to 1946; a Leica IIIb from 1946 to 1955; a Leica M3 from 1955 to 1959; and a Leicaflex from 1959 until 1992. The images that he took with the Leicaflex in Ethiopia in 1959 show the work of a skilled photographer, seriously engaged with his medium. He always sent unexposed film home to his mother in London, for developing and printing at James A. Sinclair & Co., and subsequently compiled personal albums of his journeys.

In late 1944 Thesiger was offered the opportunity to join the Middle East Anti-Locust Unit, looking for locust outbreaks in southern Arabia. Arriving in 1945, he spent the next four years traveling by camel with Bedouin companions in the remotest parts of the region, crossing the Rub al-Khali, or Empty Quarter, not once but twice. During these journeys he took numerous photographs of the desert, its landscapes, and its inhabitants. Equally important, he made lifelong friends, most notably Salim bin Kabina and Salim bin Ghabaisha, who are seen in many of his photographs. Thesiger read his paper "Desert Borderlands of Oman" at a meeting of the Royal Geographical Society in October 1949; the paper was published in *The Geographical Journal* in December 1950 along with his photographs.

During a monthlong visit to Al-Ain in April 1948, Thesiger—now known throughout Arabia as Mubarak bin London, "the blessed one from London," a nickname given him by his Bedouin companions—met Sheikh Zayed bin Sultan al-Nahyan. When

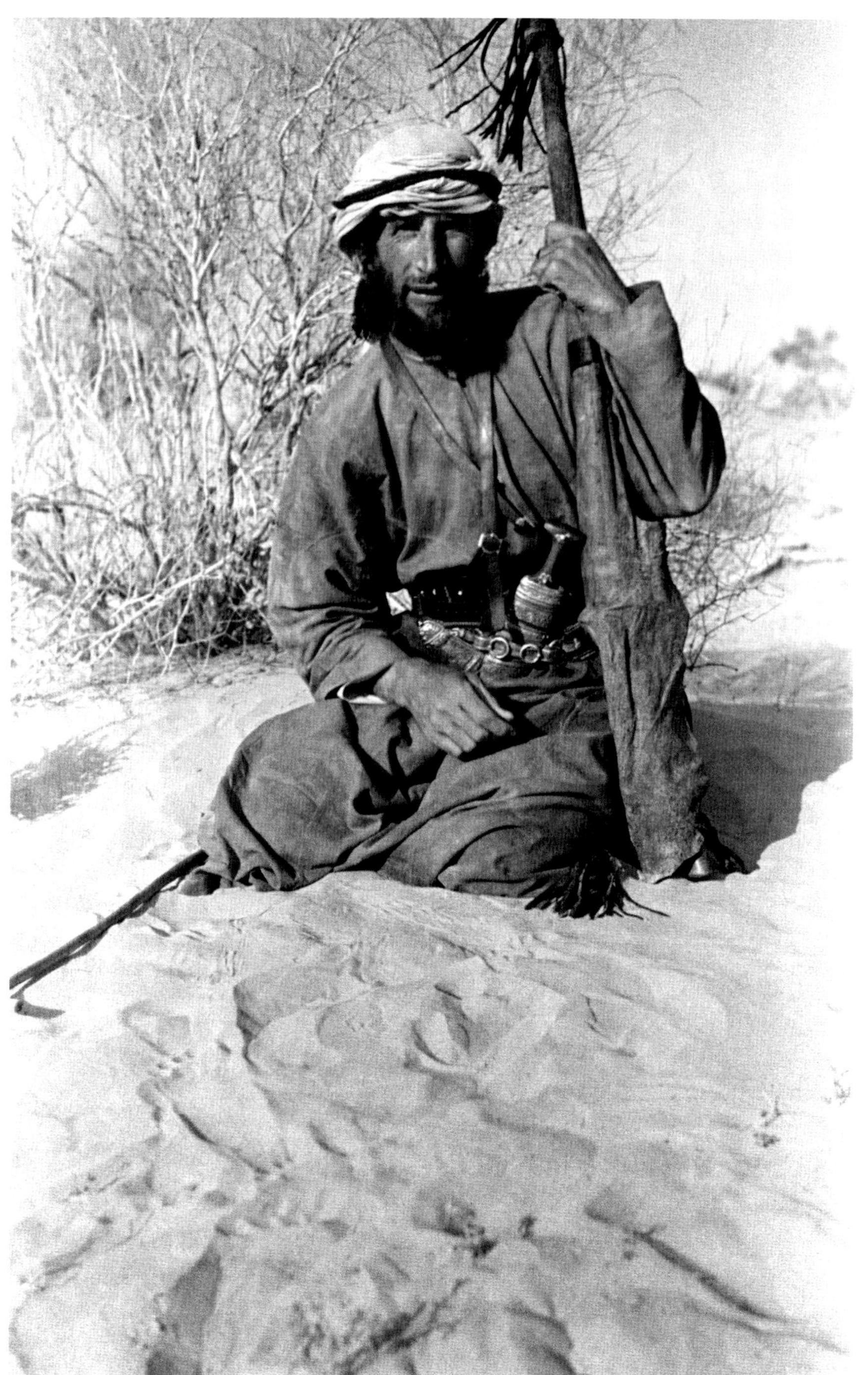

Thesiger returned at the end of the year, he stayed for three weeks with Sheikh Zayed, during which time they camped and hawked with peregrine falcons in the desert. The portraits that Thesiger took of Sheikh Zayed during this period are some of the best known, and most admired, of all the images taken of the man who would later become the first president of the United Arab Emirates. The friendship between the two men was an enduring one. In 1977 Thesiger visited the UAE at Sheikh Zayed's invitation, after an absence of some twenty-five years. He then returned again, in 1990, to open an exhibition of his photographs in Abu Dhabi.

Wilfred Thesiger's life in the Rub al-Khali, along with his subsequent book, *Arabian Sands* (1959), which detailed his travels across the desert, have been widely celebrated in Oman. Thesiger received many awards for his accomplishments, including a knighthood from Queen Elizabeth in 1965. Sir Wilfred died in London in 2003. In honor of his memory, through the generosity of Sultan Qaboos, the Sultan of Oman, the Royal Geographical Society—which awarded Thesiger its Founder's Medal in 1948 for his travels in Arabia—offers two annual grants for geographical research in the arid regions of the world. In 2004 the British government accepted all of Thesiger's thirty-eight thousand negatives and seventy-one personal albums as art in lieu of an inheritance tax and allocated them to the University of Oxford's Pitt Rivers Museum, where they now form the Thesiger Collection.

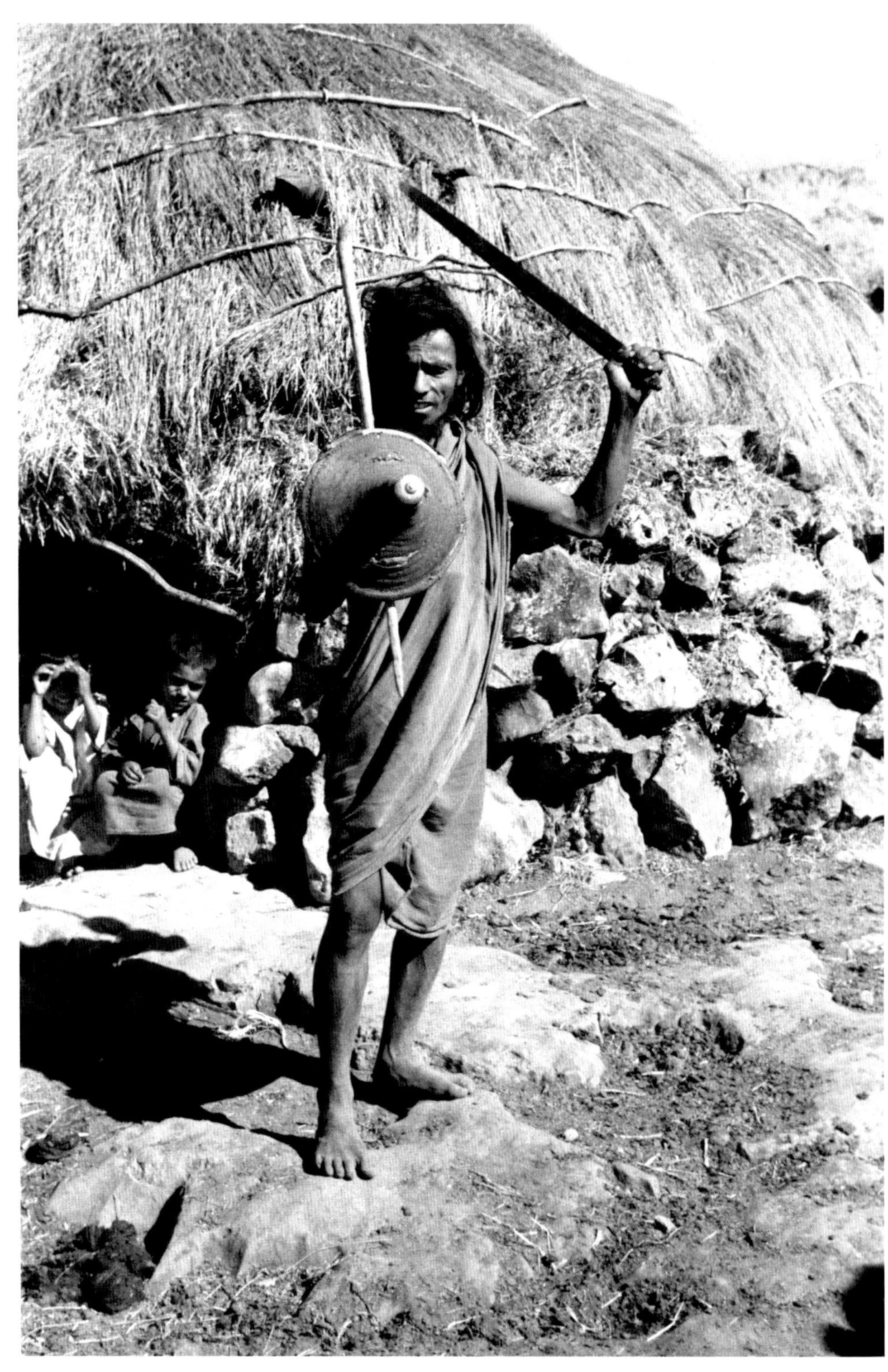

Man in Jabal Qara, mountains
near Salalah, in Dhofar, 1945

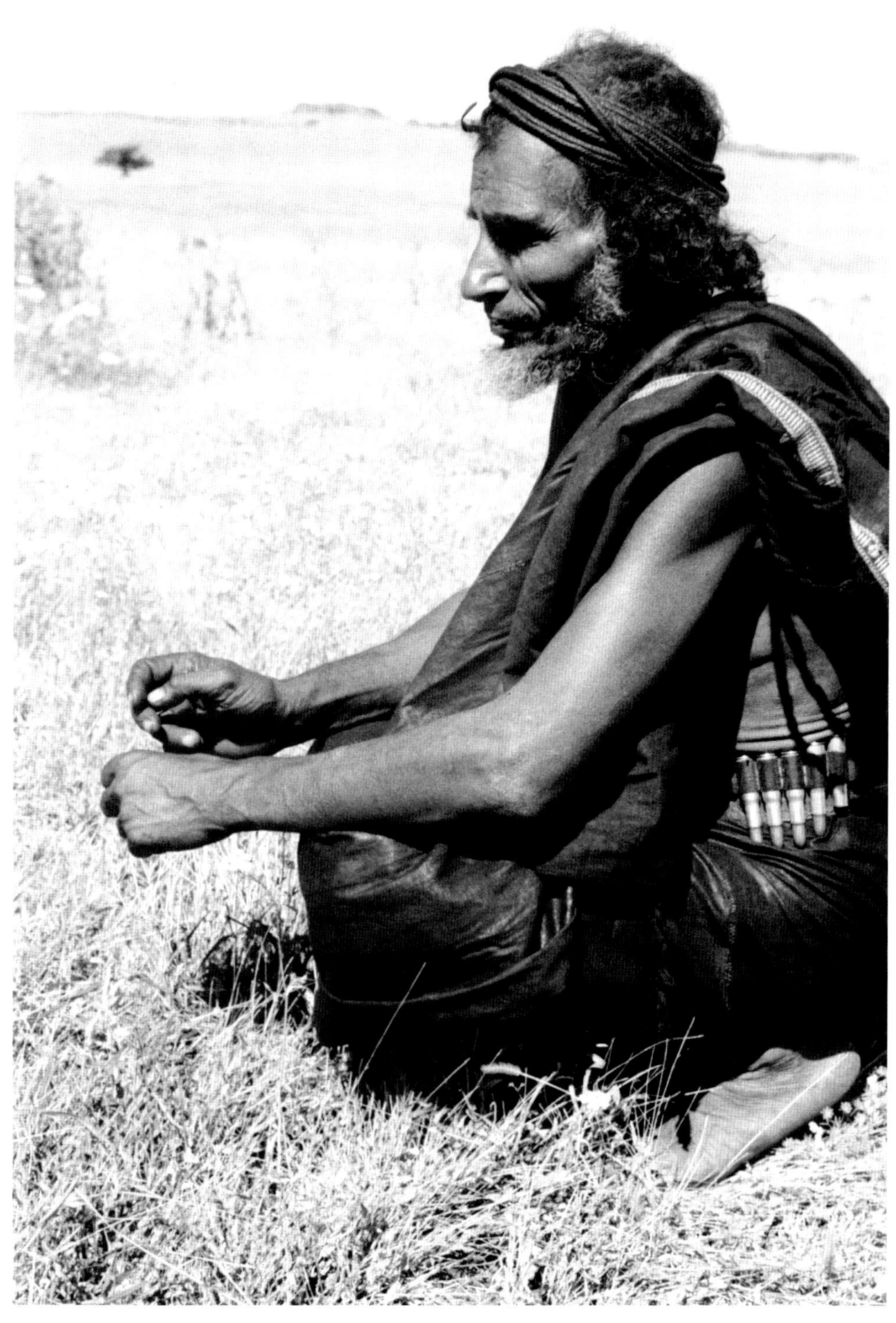

Qara tribesman
from Jabal Qara, 1945

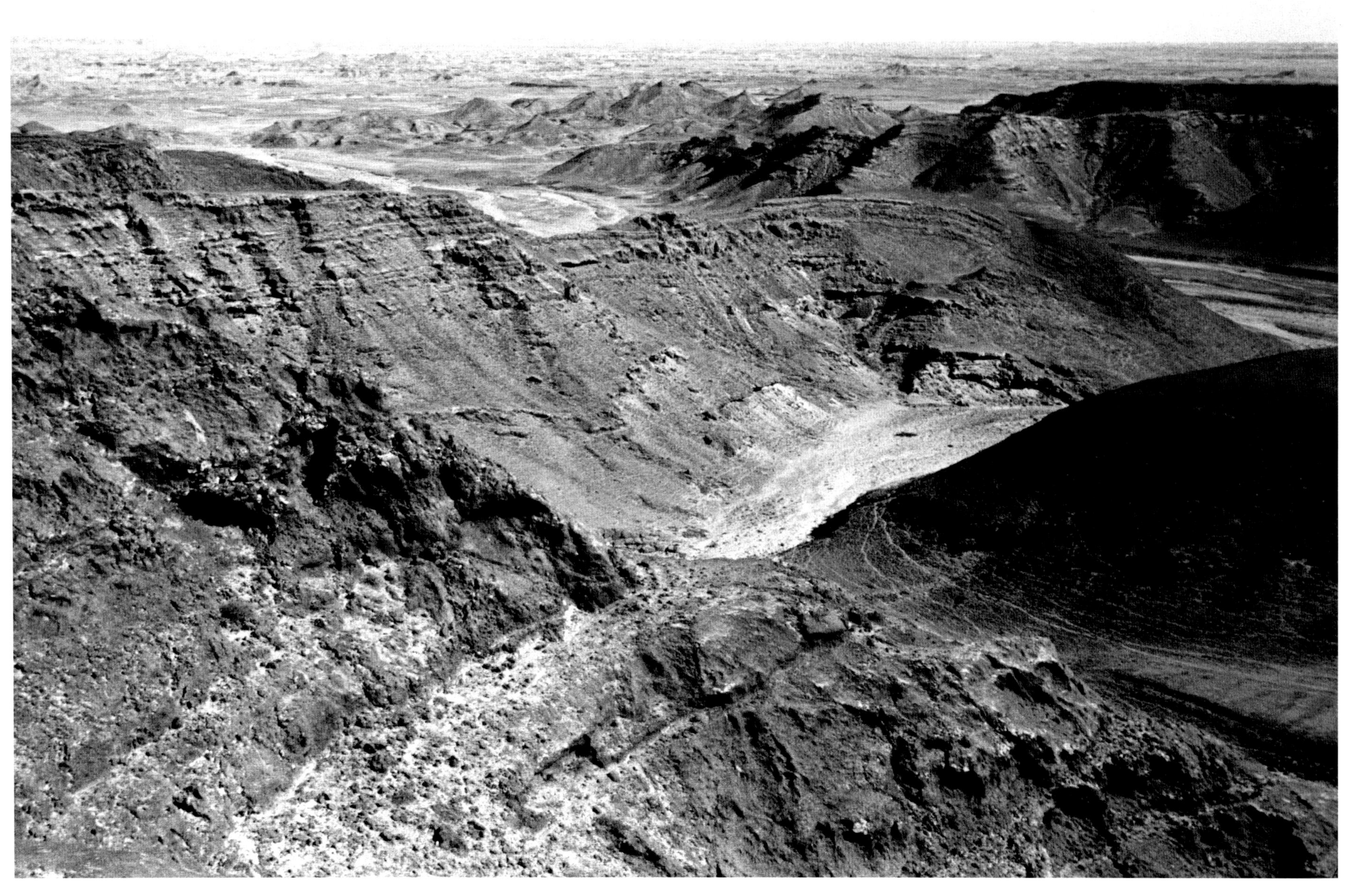

Landscape, Jabal Qara, 1945

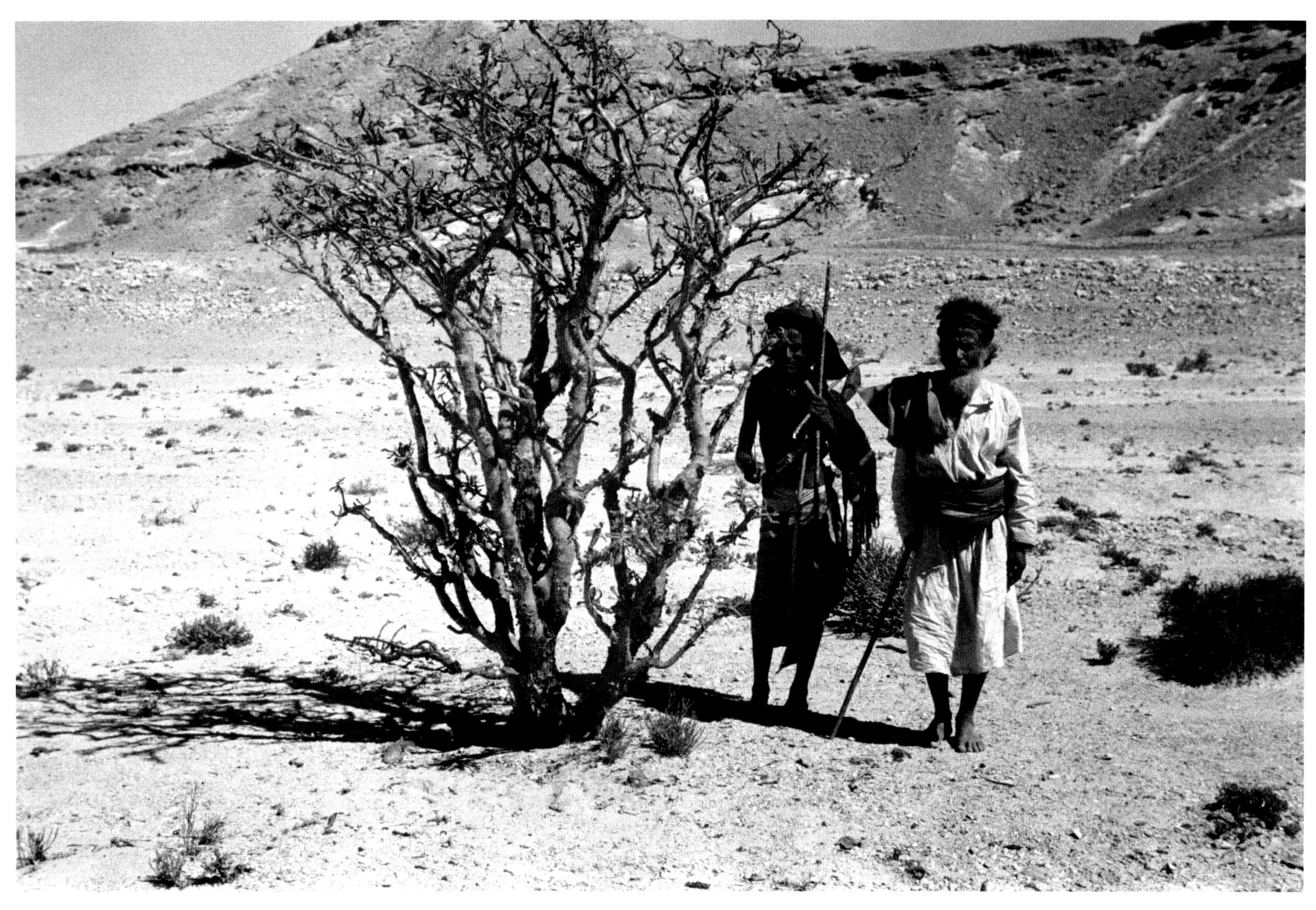

Two men beside a frankincense tree, northern slope of Jabal Qara, 1945

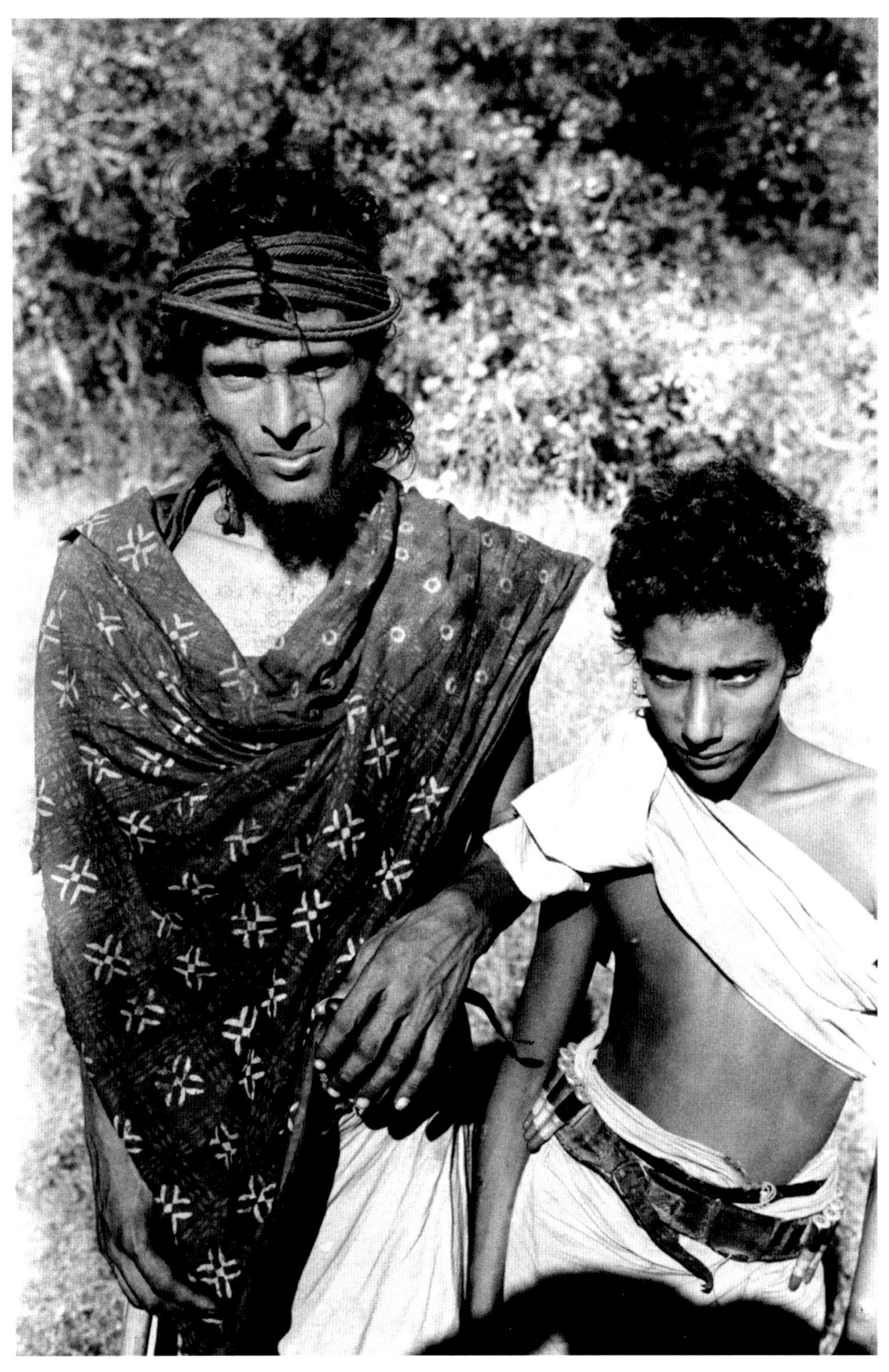

Man and boy of the Qara tribe,
Jabal Qara, 1945

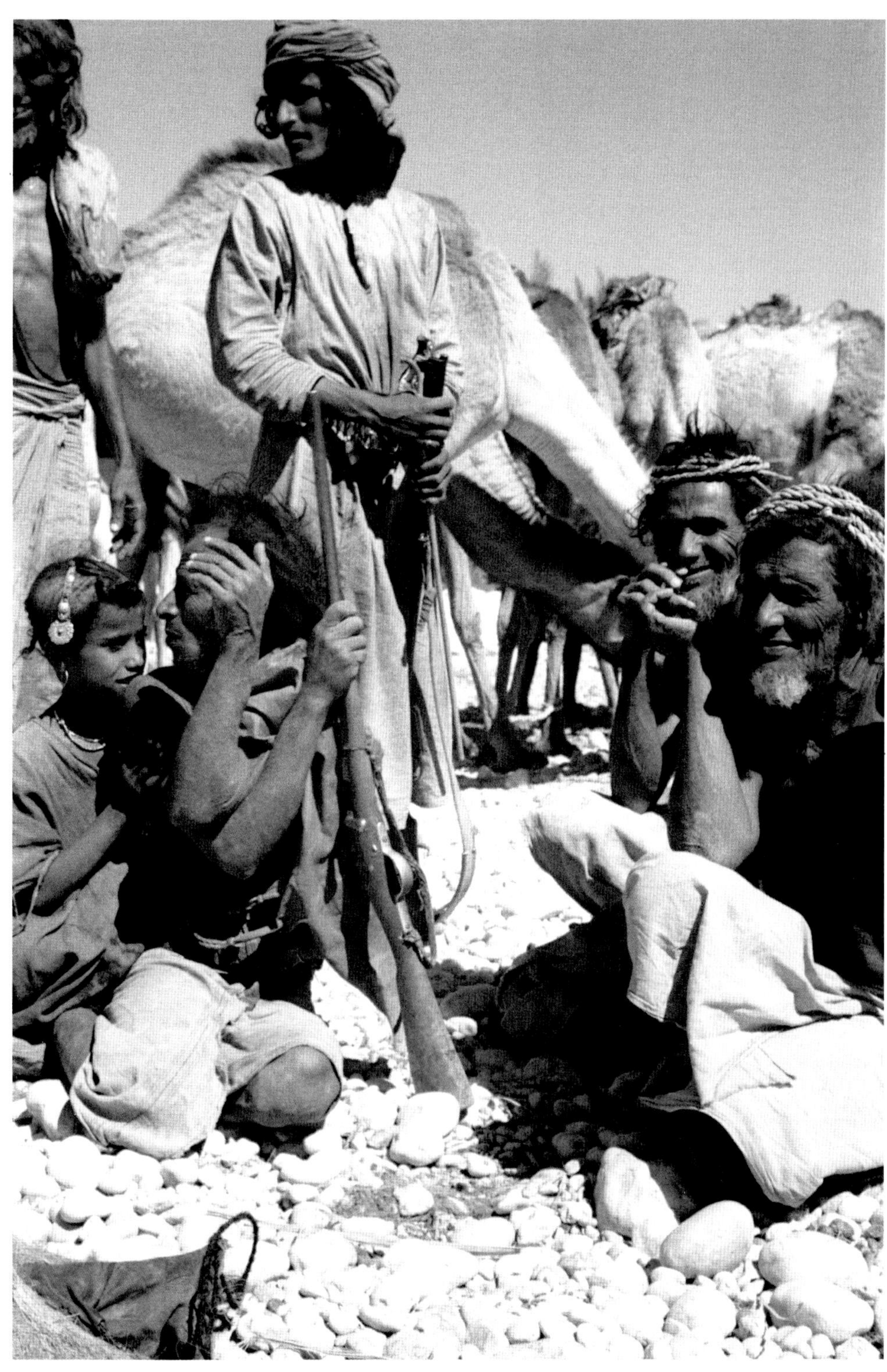

Members of the Mahra tribe, 1946

Salim bin Kabina, Ramlat al-Wahiba
(Wahiba Sands), 1946

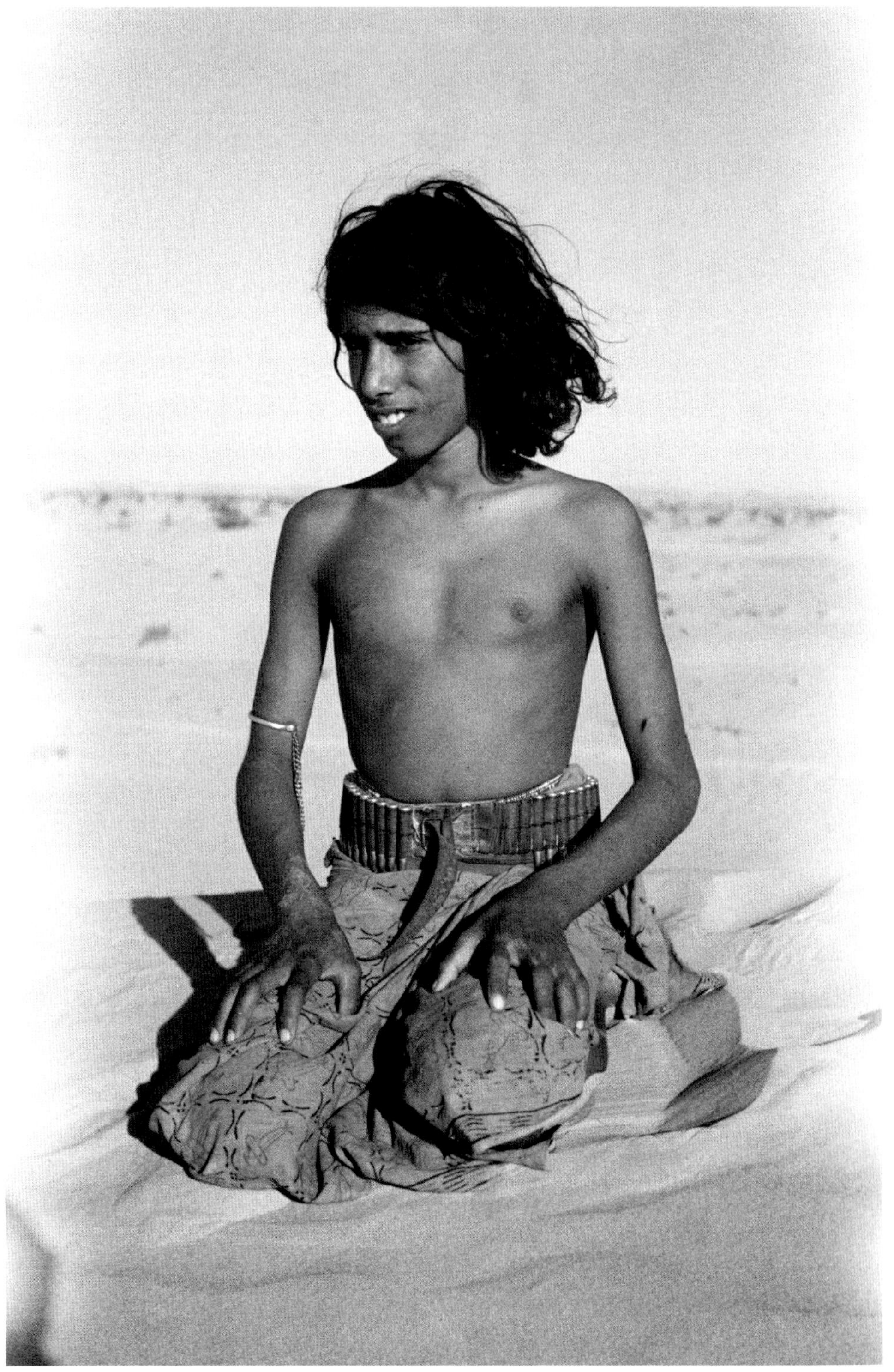

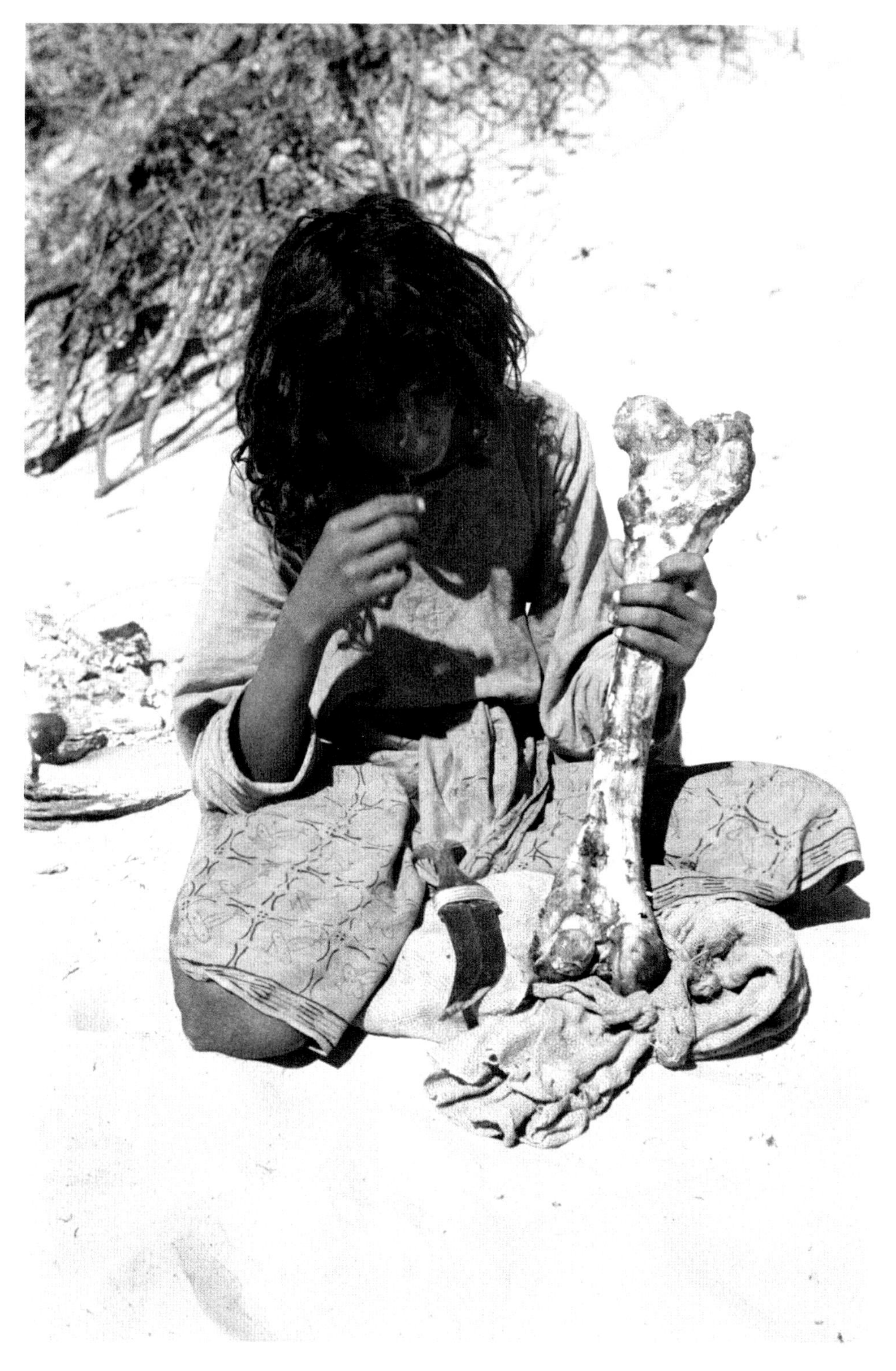

Salim bin Kabina stripping meat,
Ramlat al-Wahiba, 1946

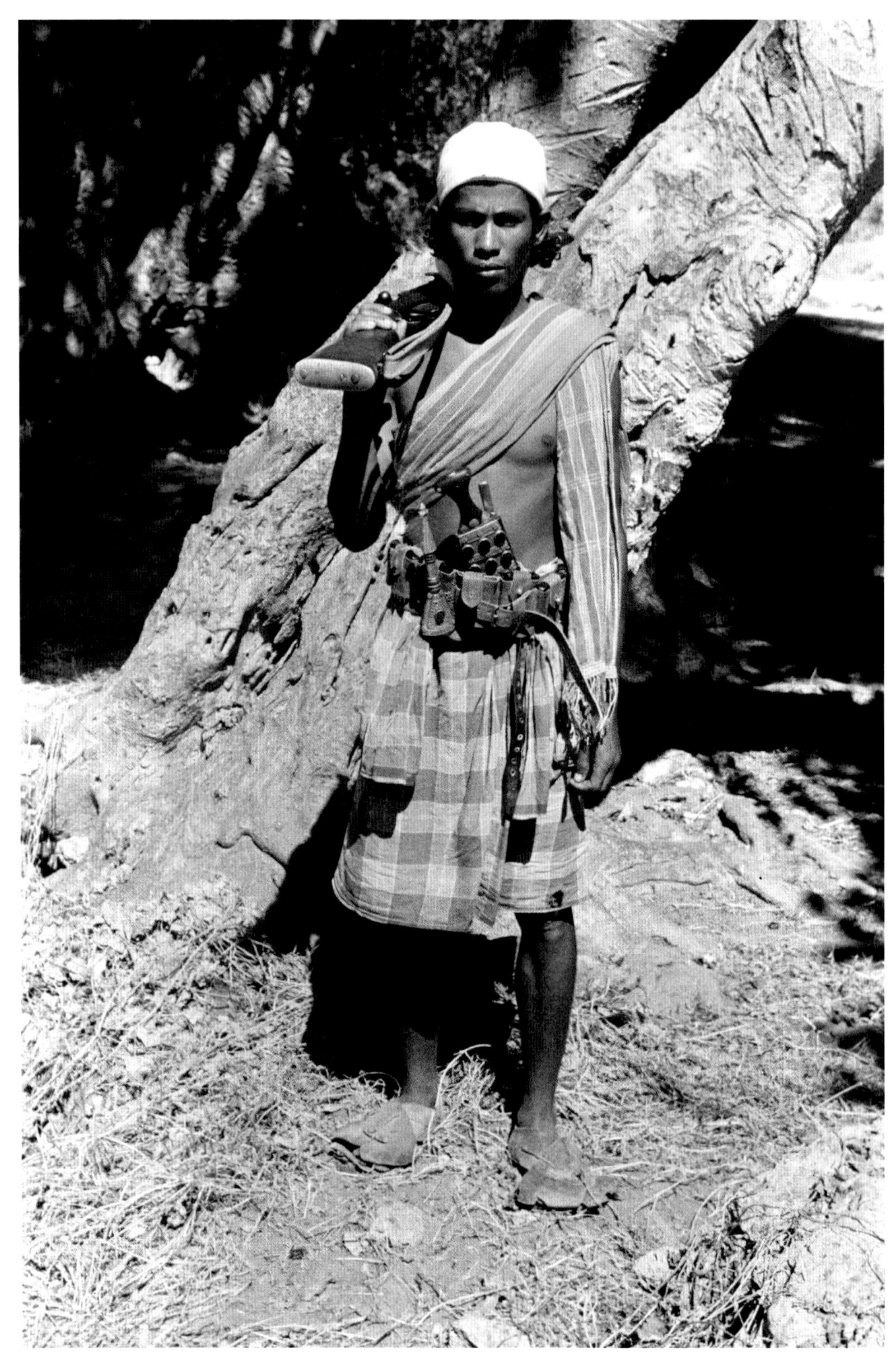

Man from Aden, 1945

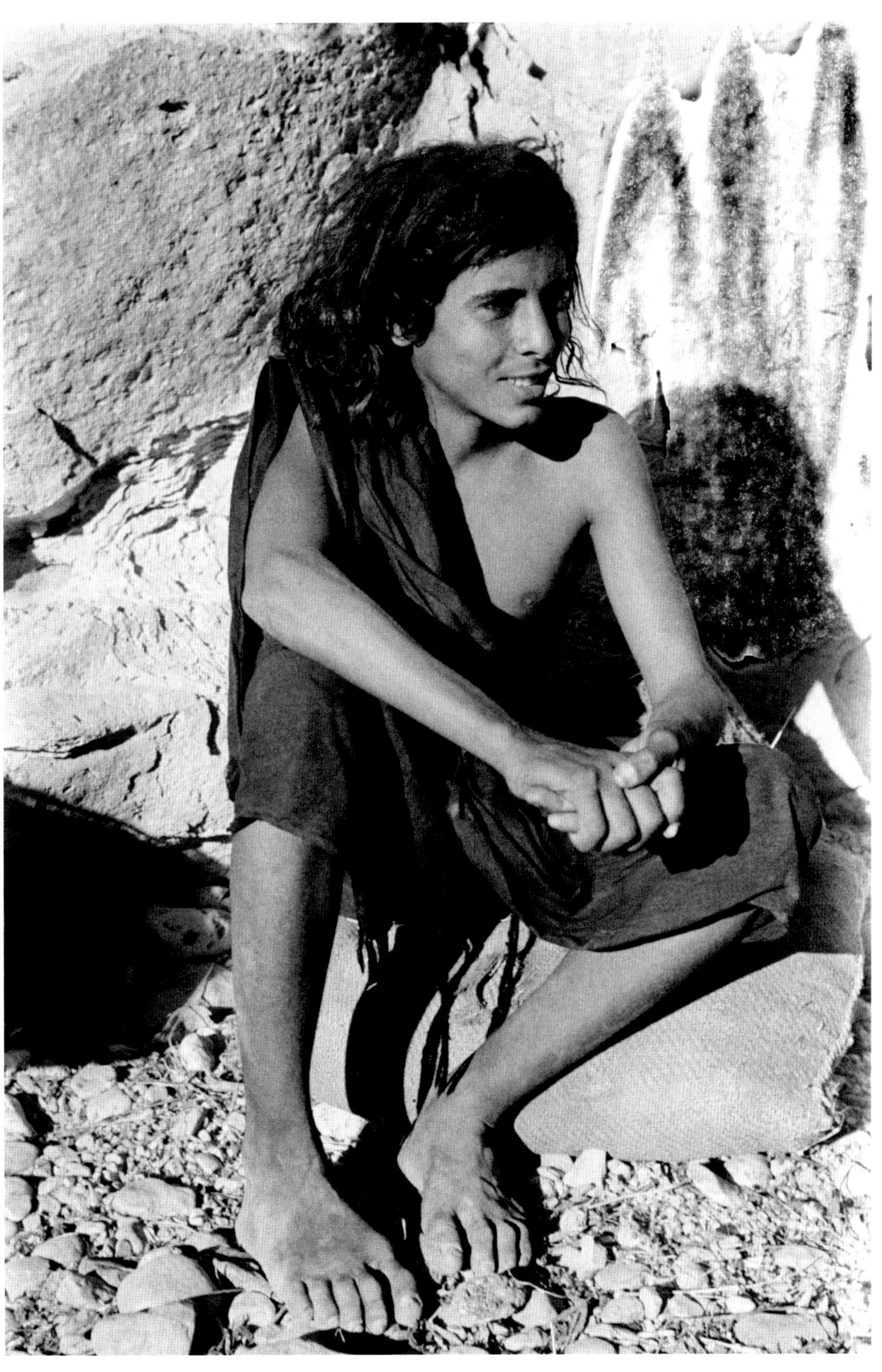

Salim bin Ghabaisha, Jabal Qara, 1947

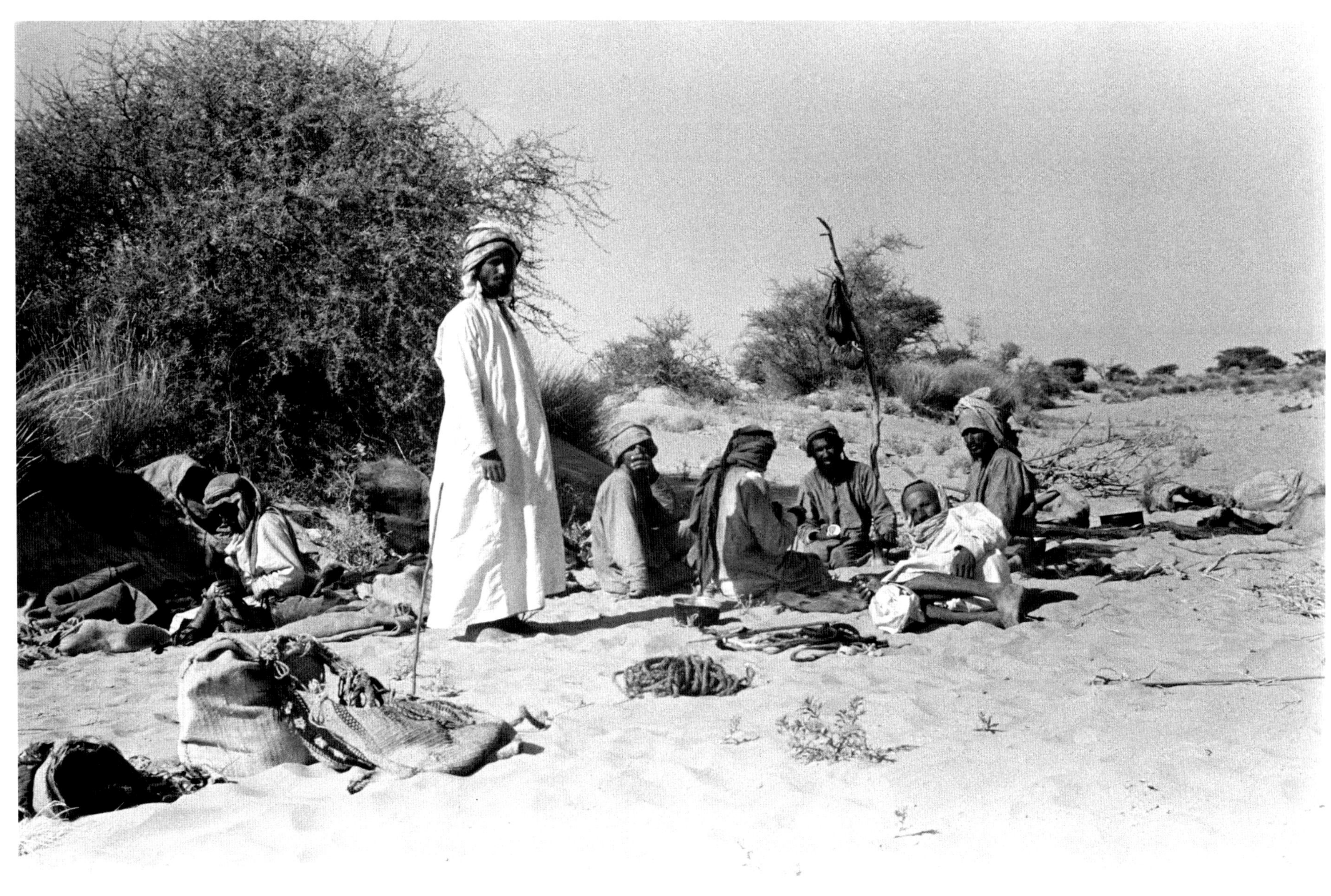

Thesiger's party making camp, Wadi al-Ain, 1949

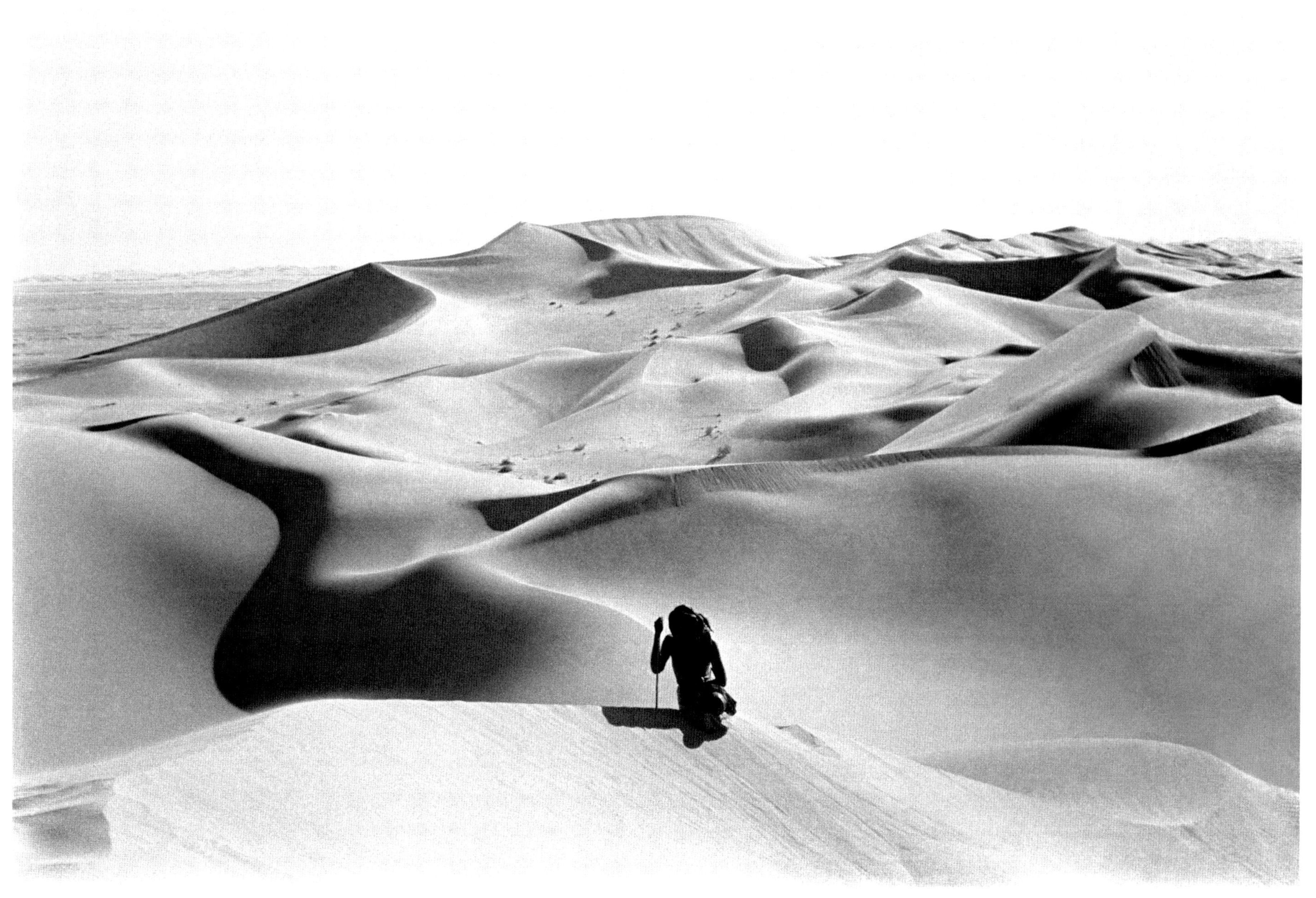

Desert landscape, Oman, 1949

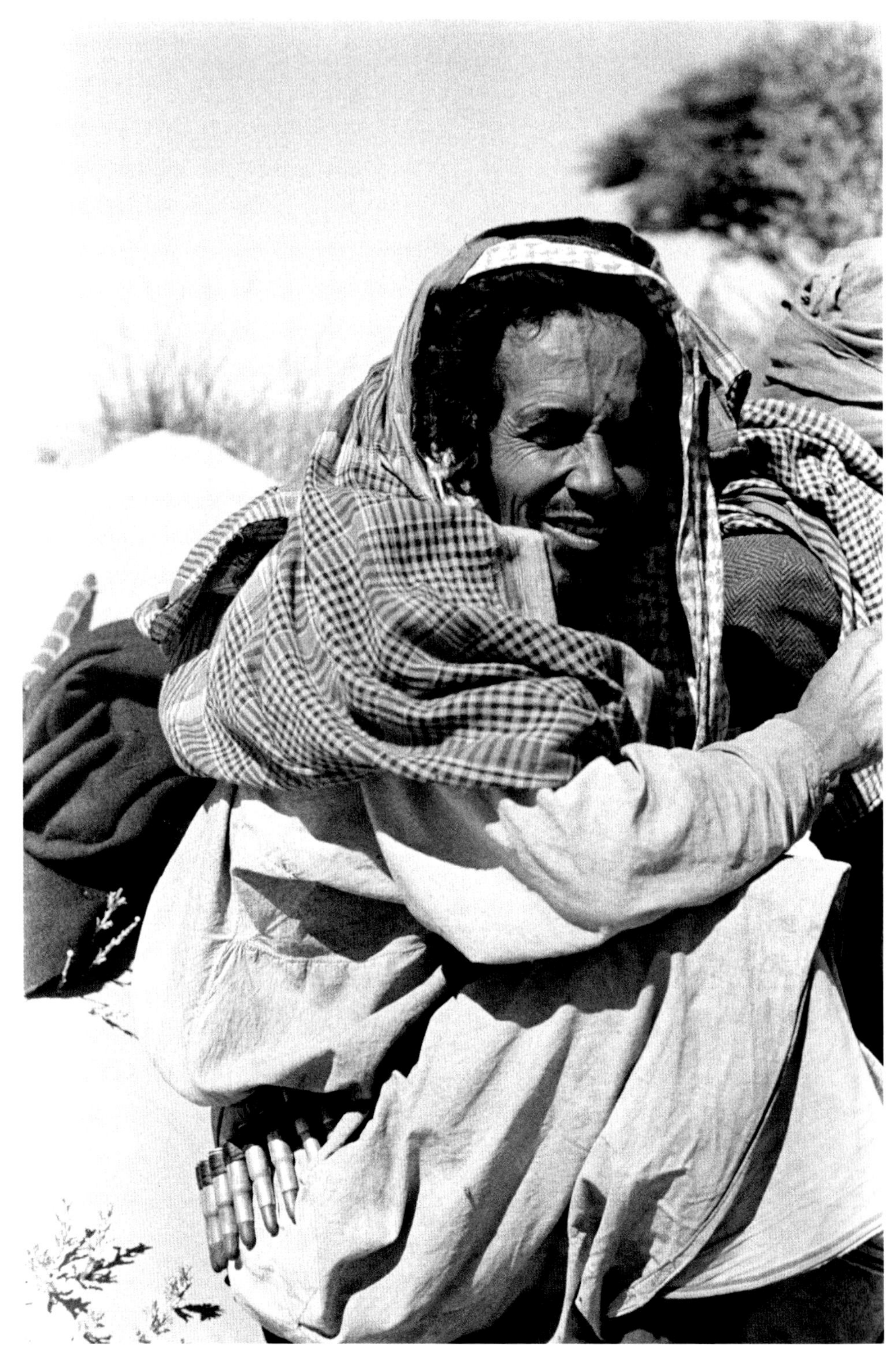

Man of the Duru tribe,
Wadi al-Ain, 1949

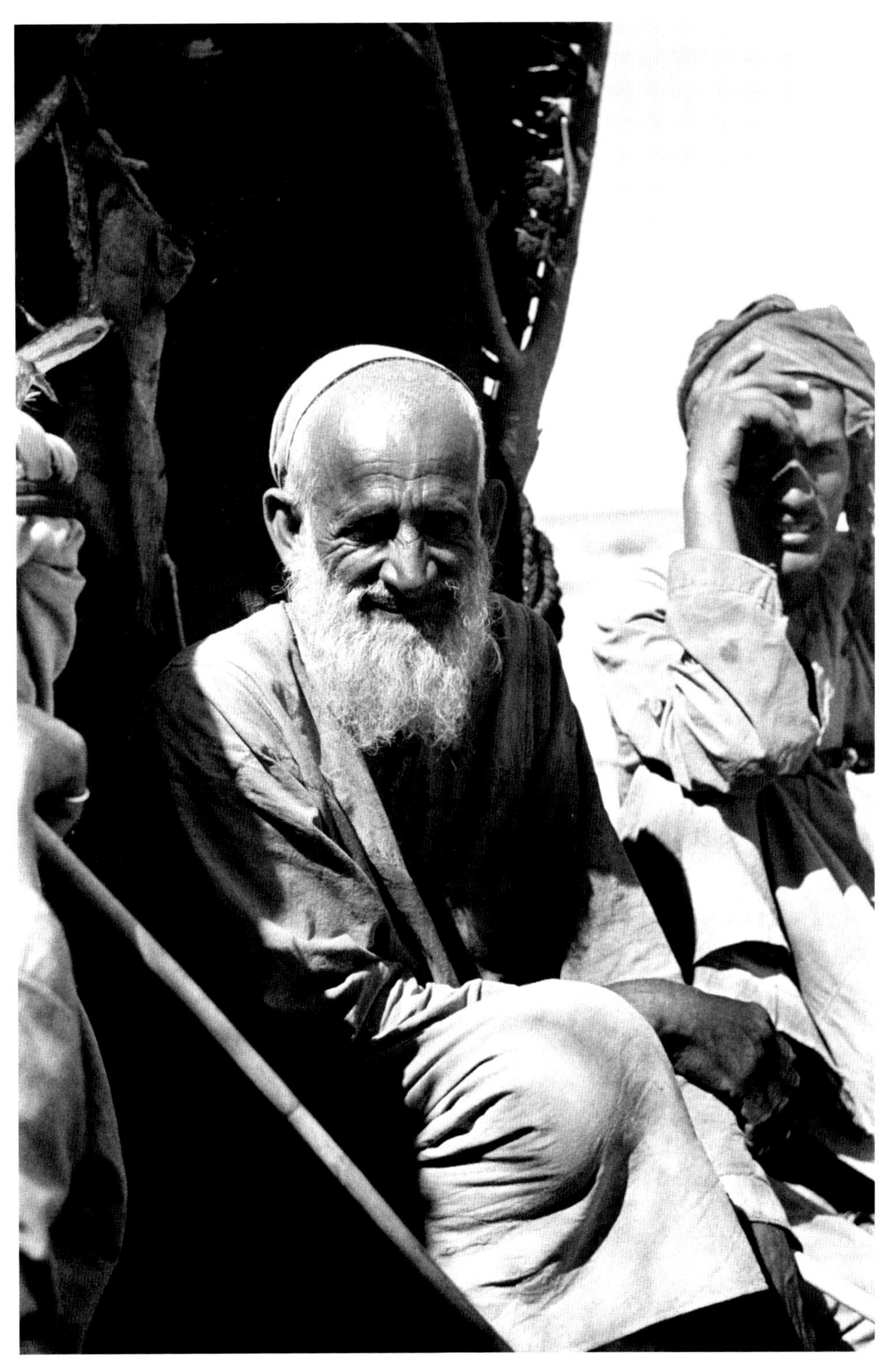

Old man of the Wahiba tribe,
Wadi Halfayn, 1949

Man of the Wahiba tribe,
Ramlat al-Wahiba, 1949

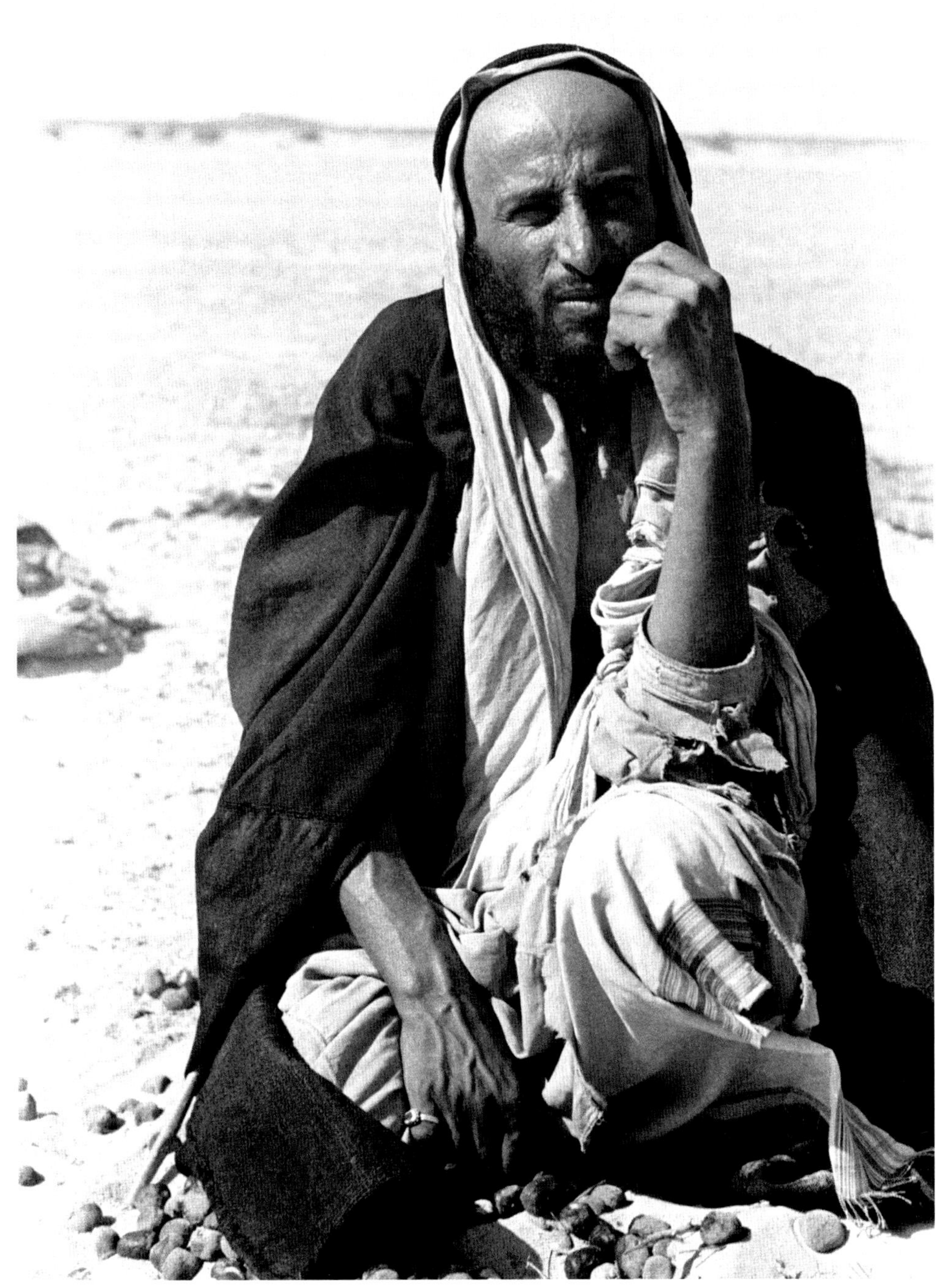

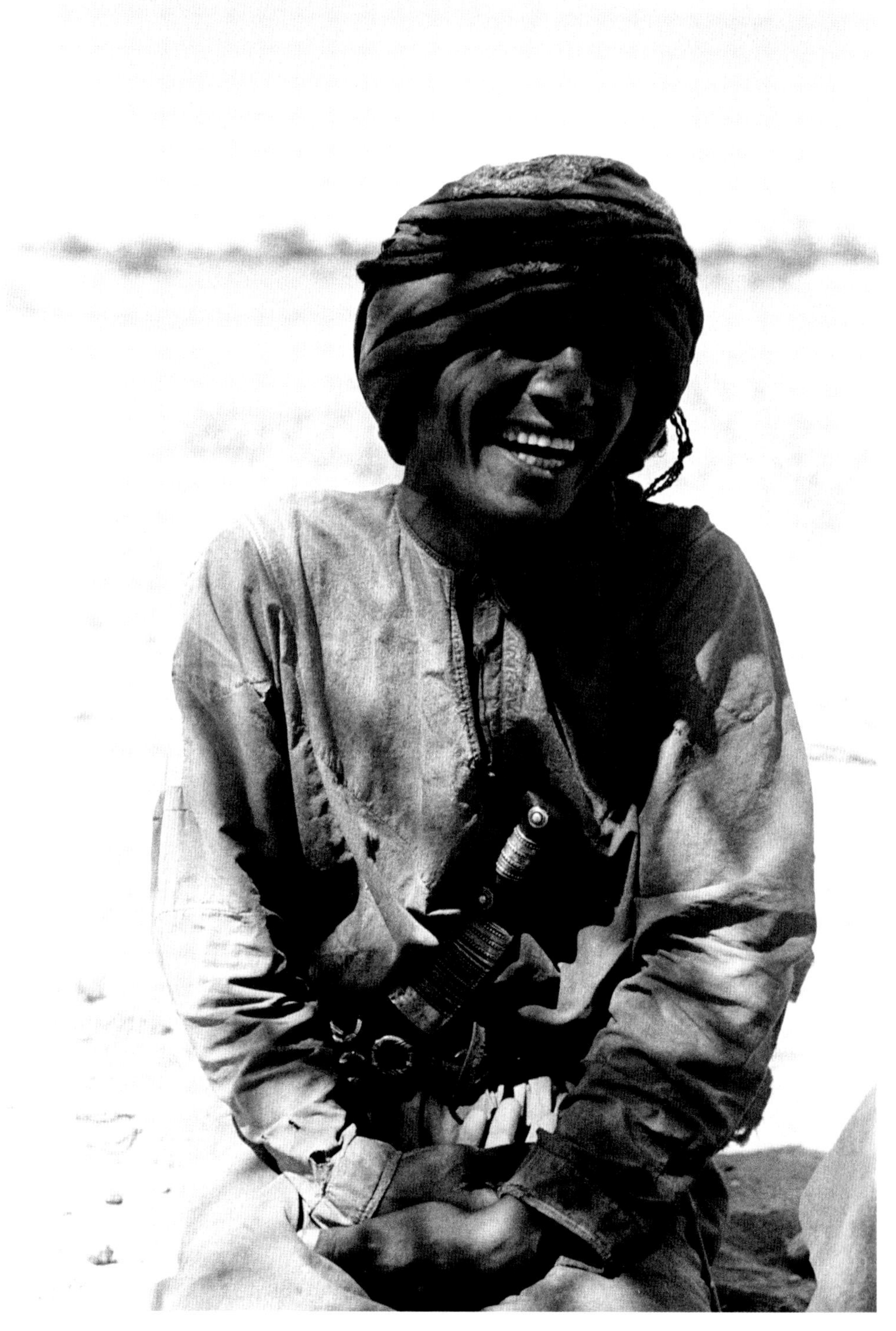

Young man of the Wahiba,
Wadi Andam, 1949

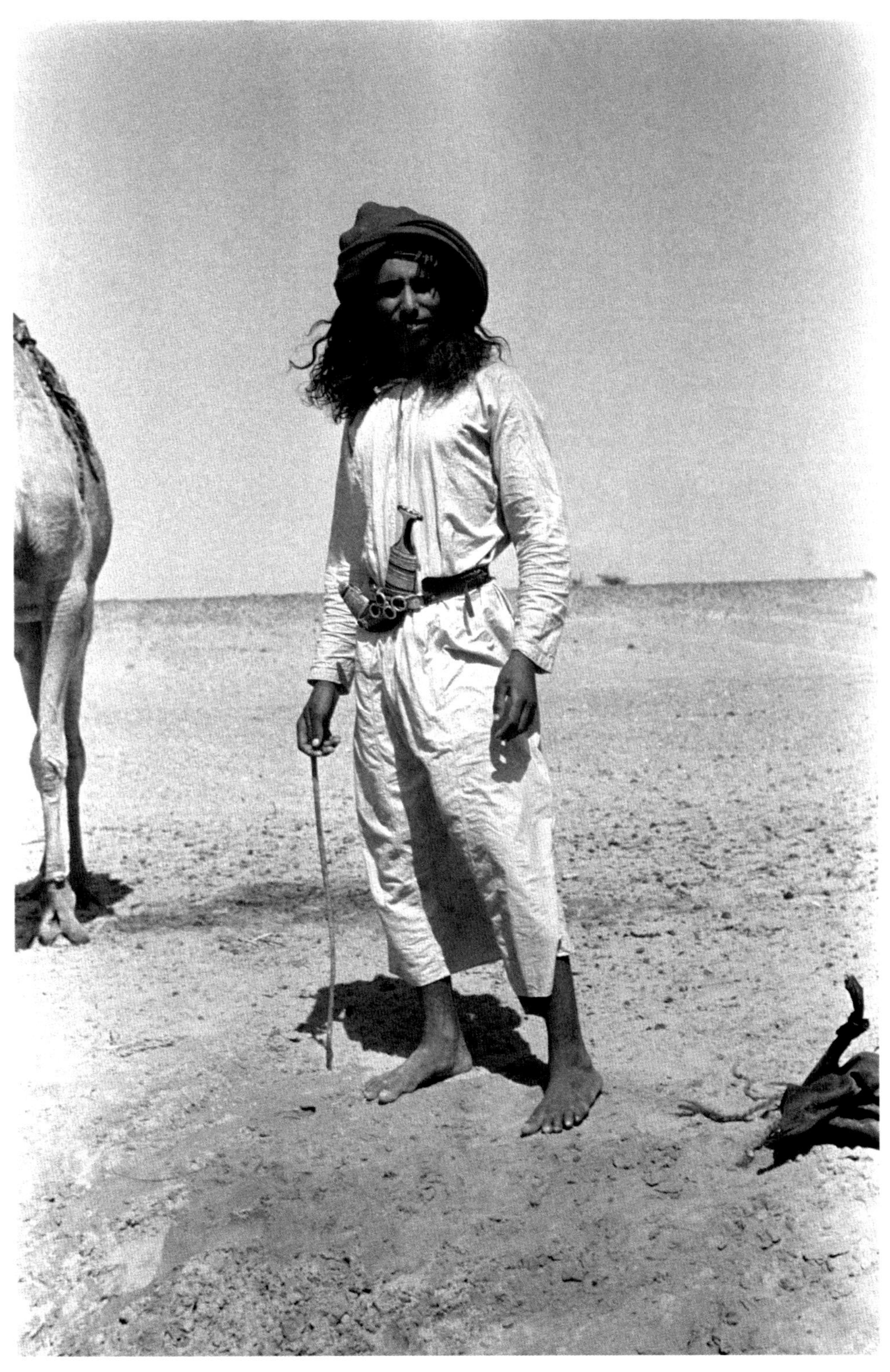

Salim bin Kabina,
Ramlat al-Wahiba, 1949

Girl of the Wahiba at a well,
Wadi Halfayn, 1949

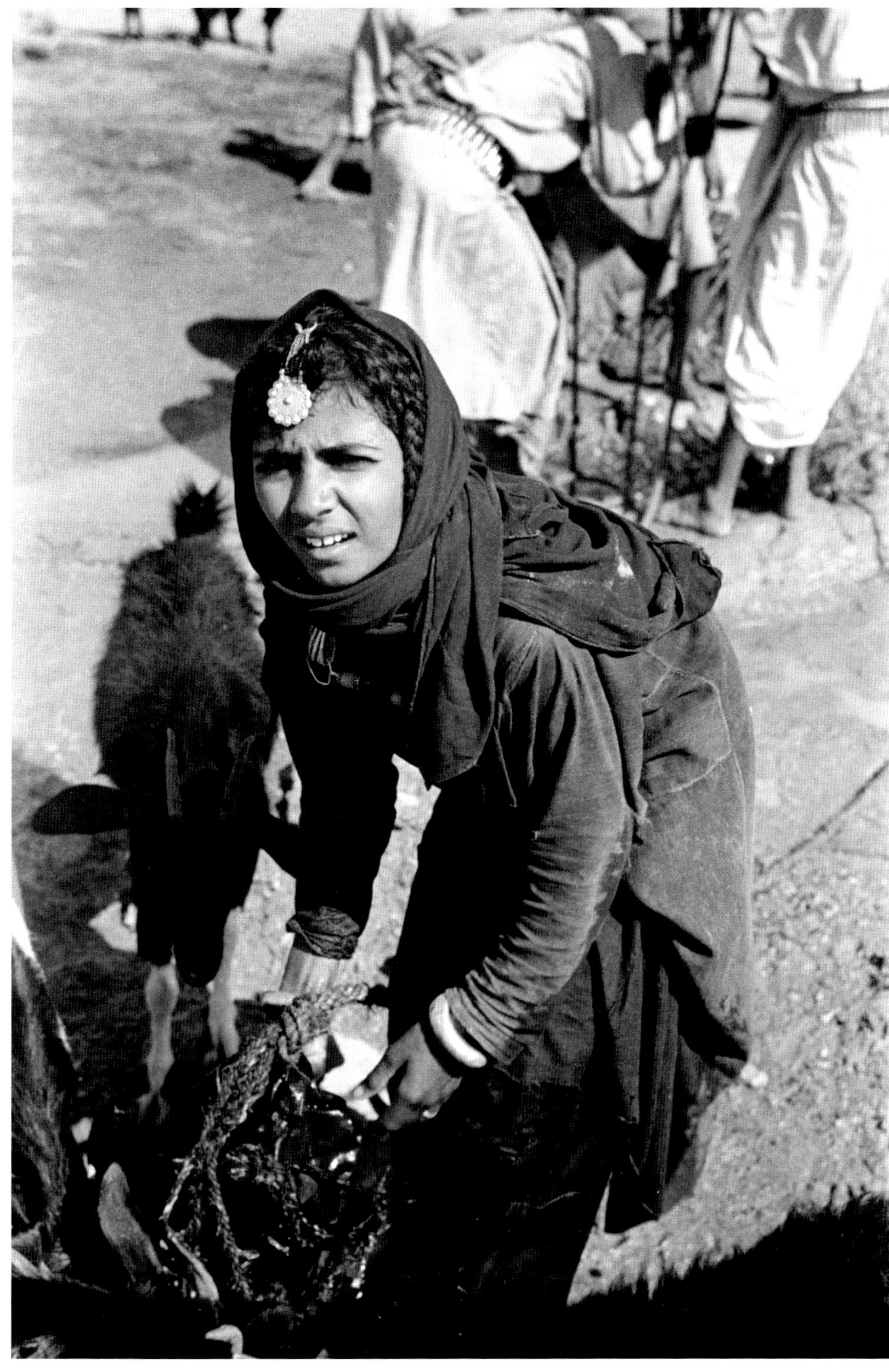

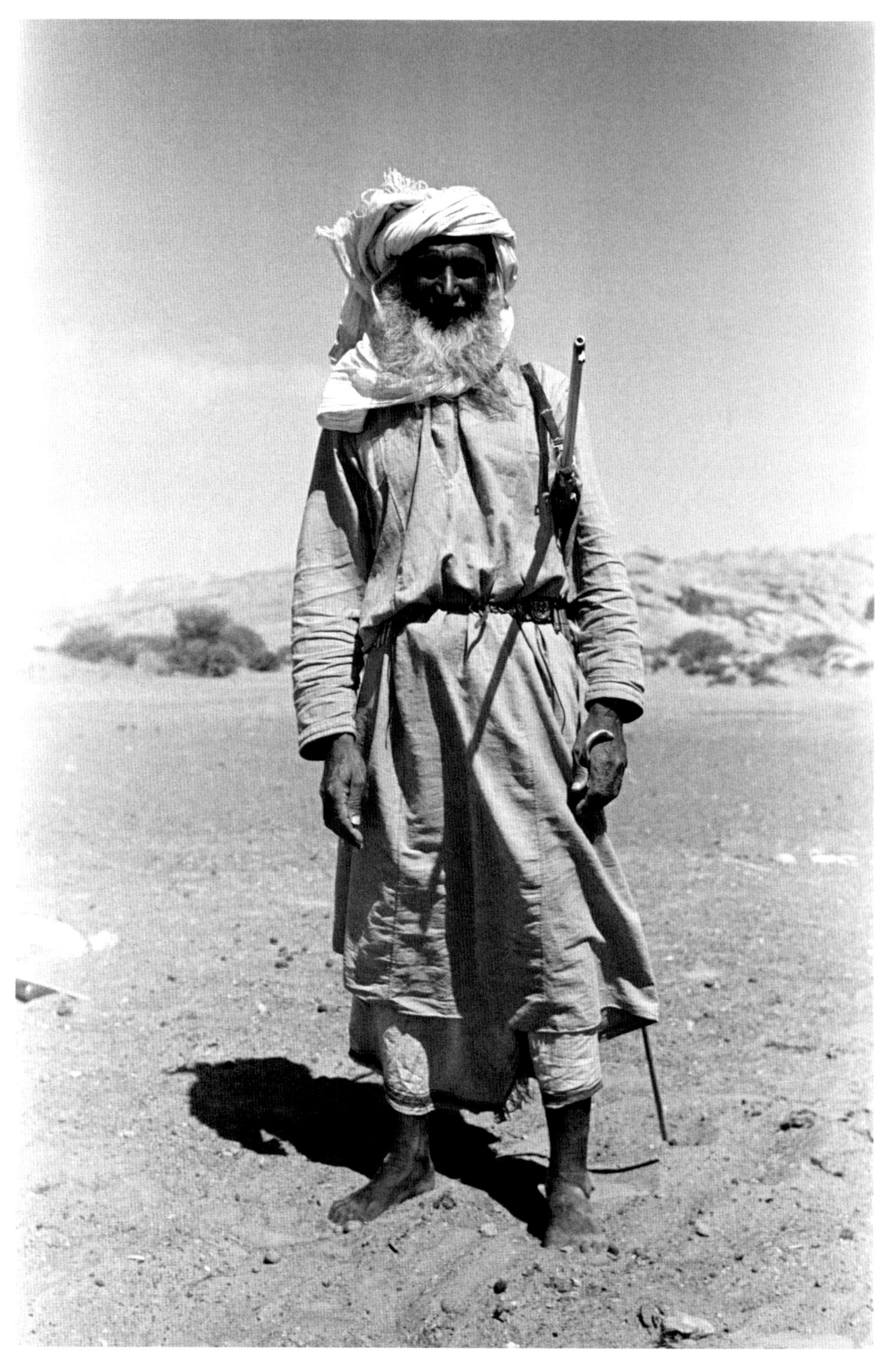

Representative of the Imam
of Oman, Jabal Hafit, 1949

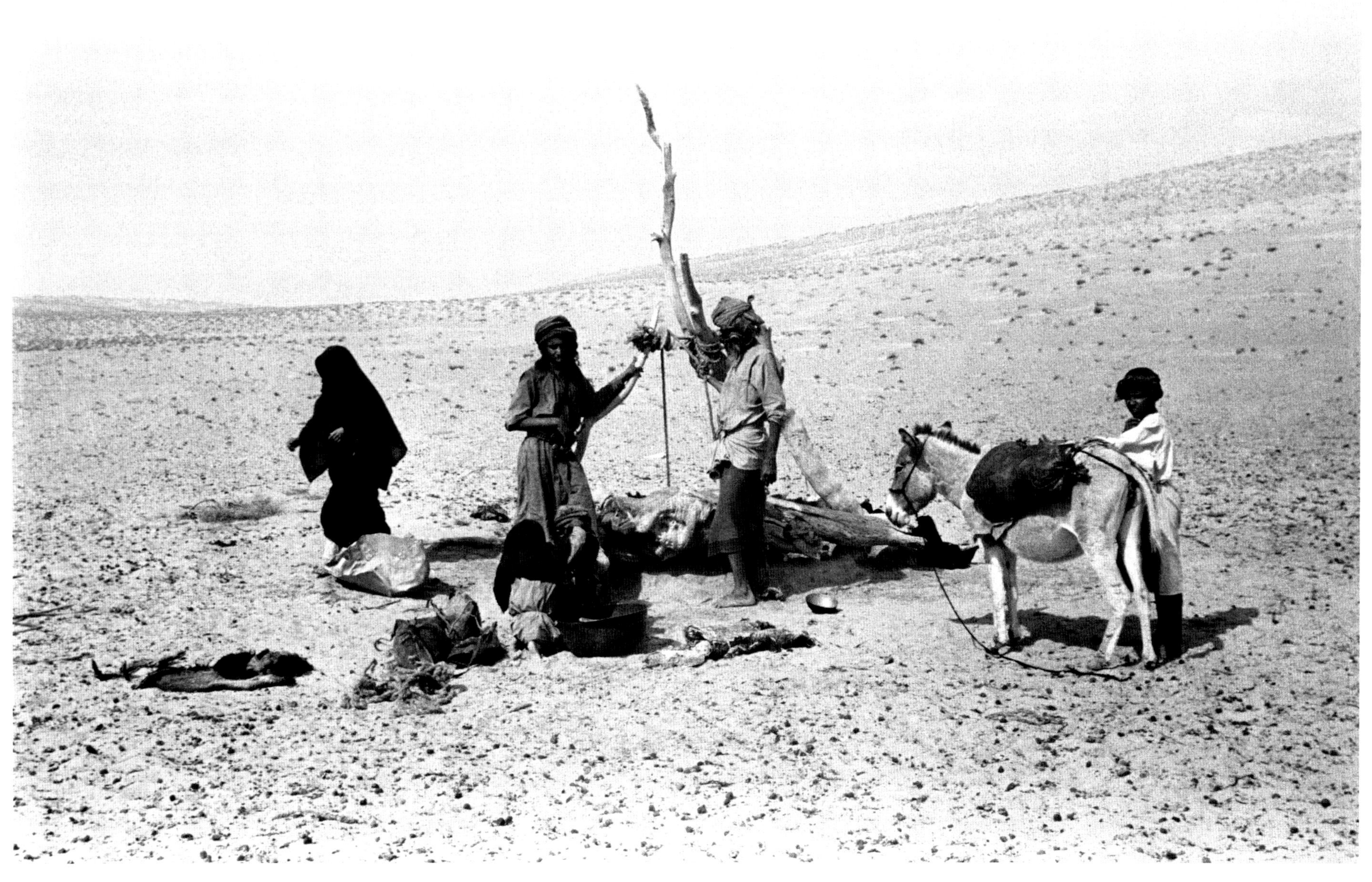

People at Tawi Harian well, Ramlat al-Wahiba, 1949

Girl of the Wahiba at a well,
Wadi Halfayn, 1949

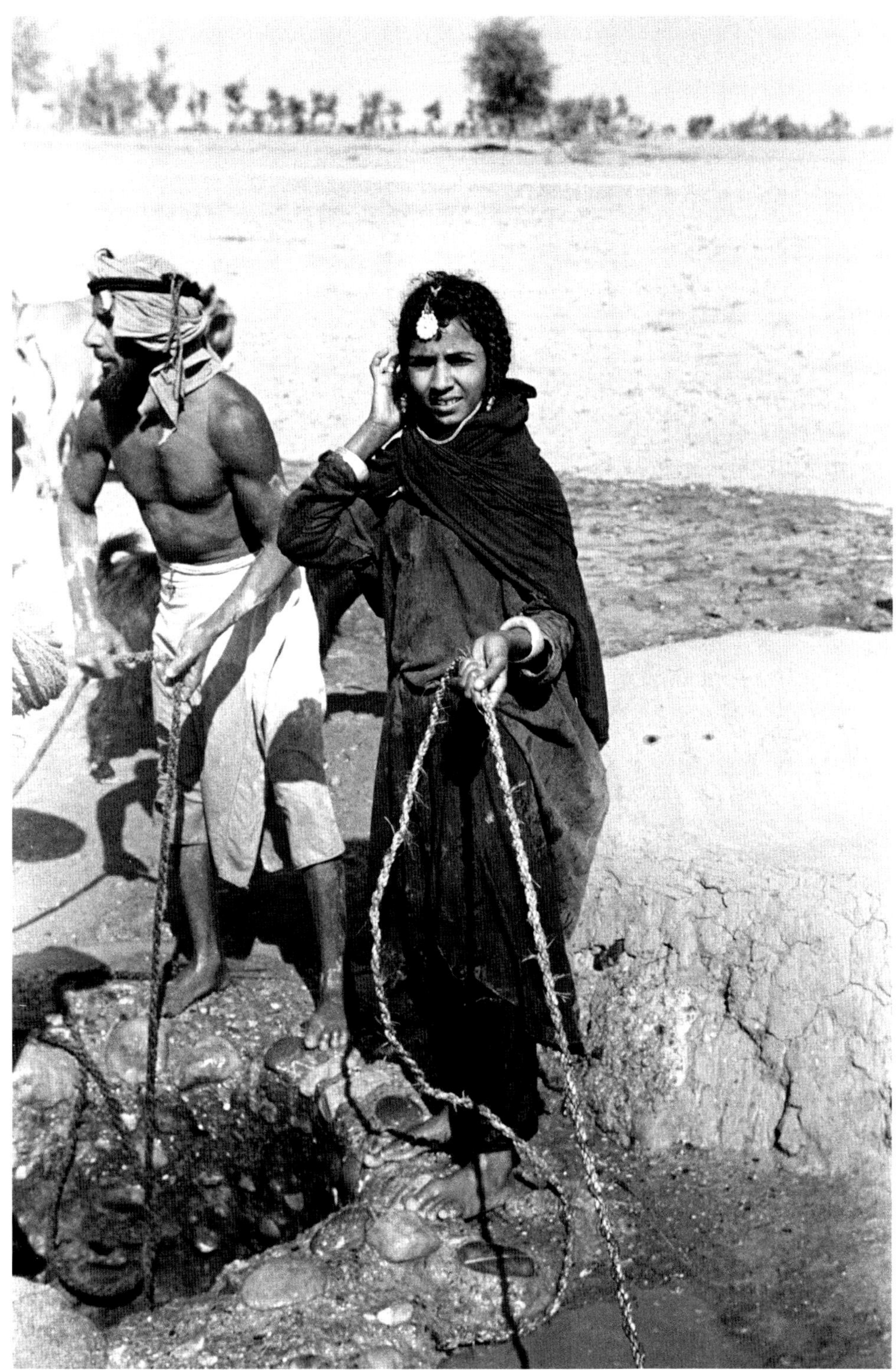

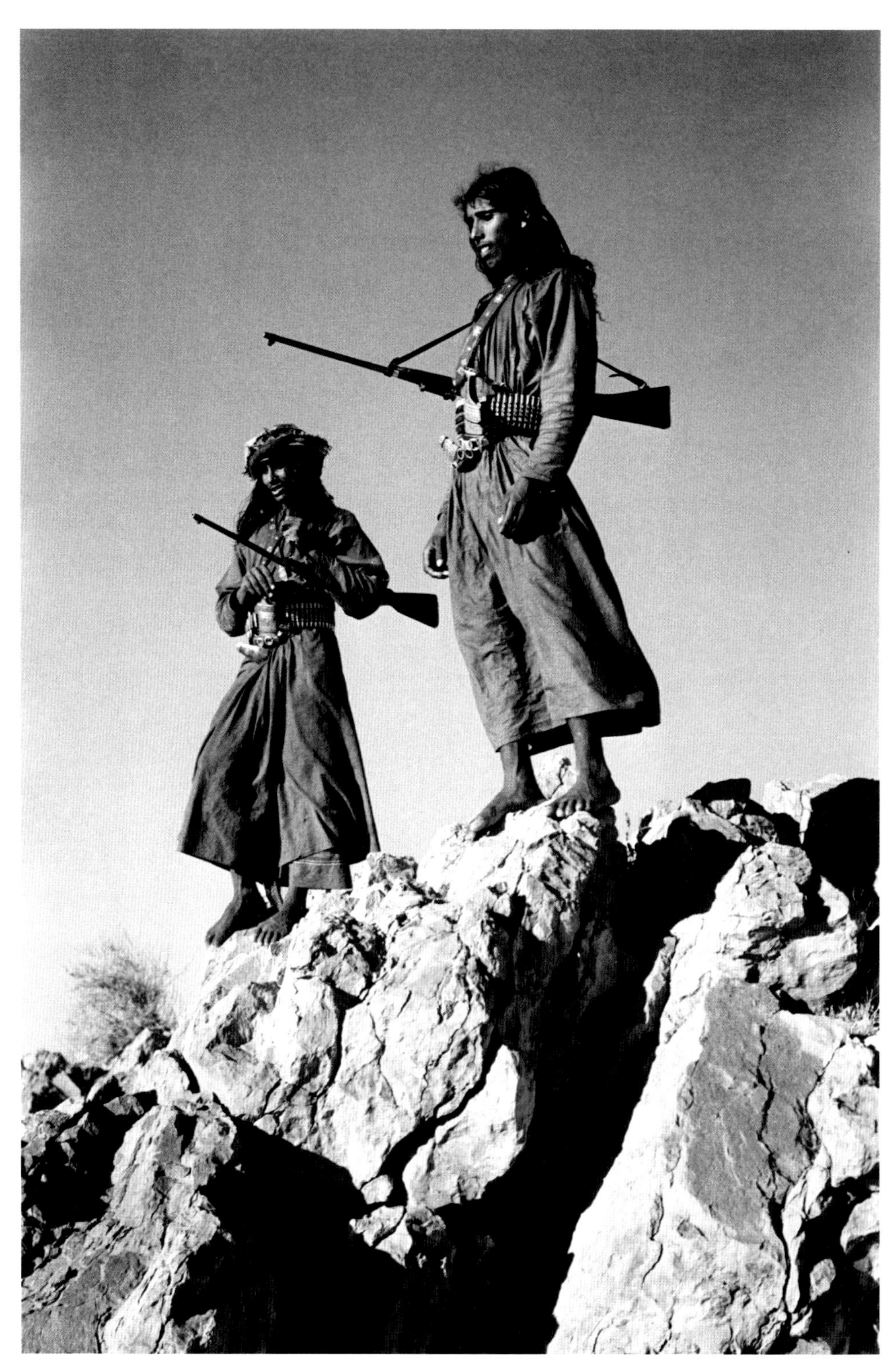

Salim bin Ghabaisha and Salim
bin Kabina, Ras al-Khaimah, 1950

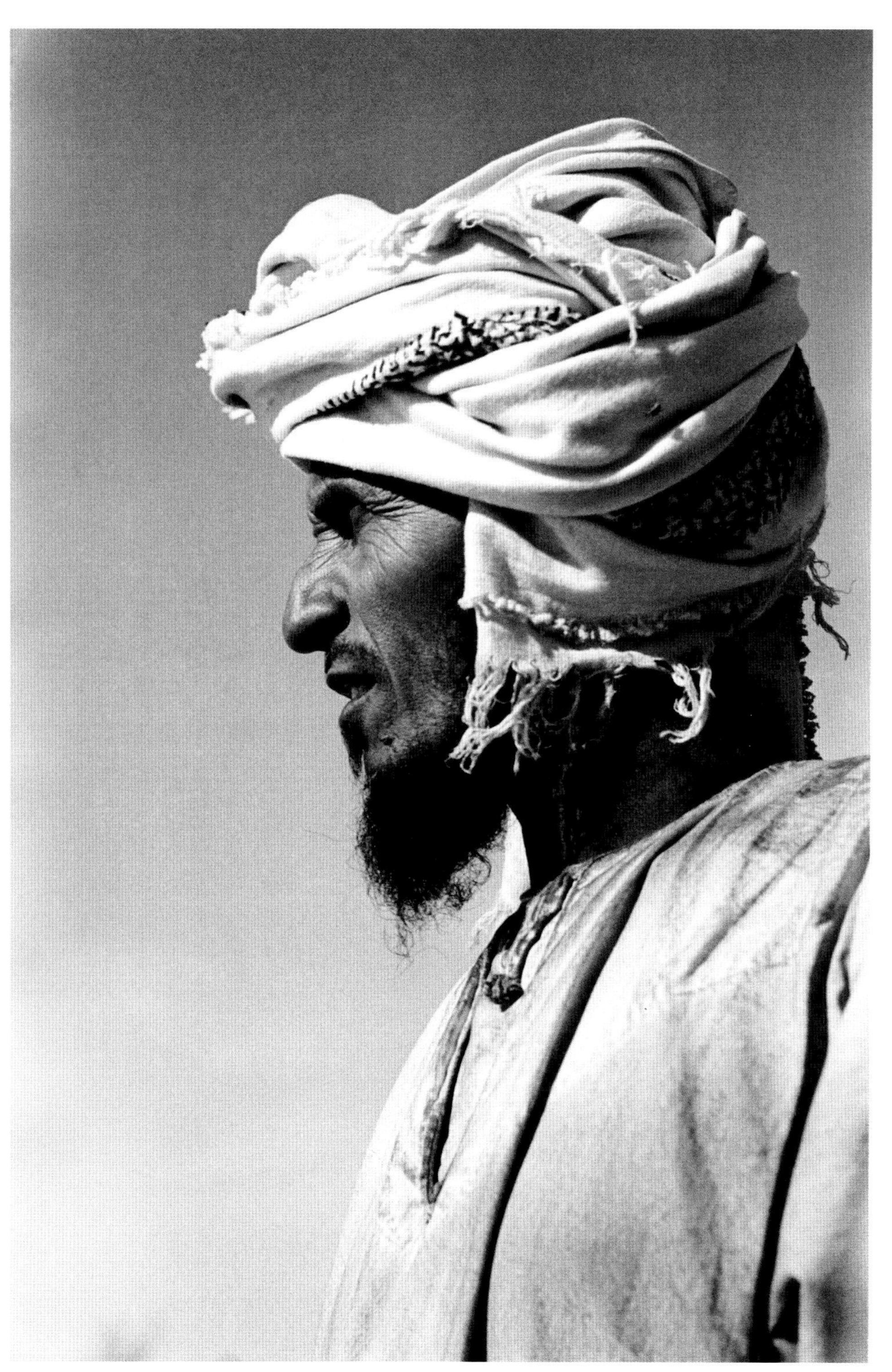

Huaishil, a sheikh of the
Duru tribe, Oman, 1950

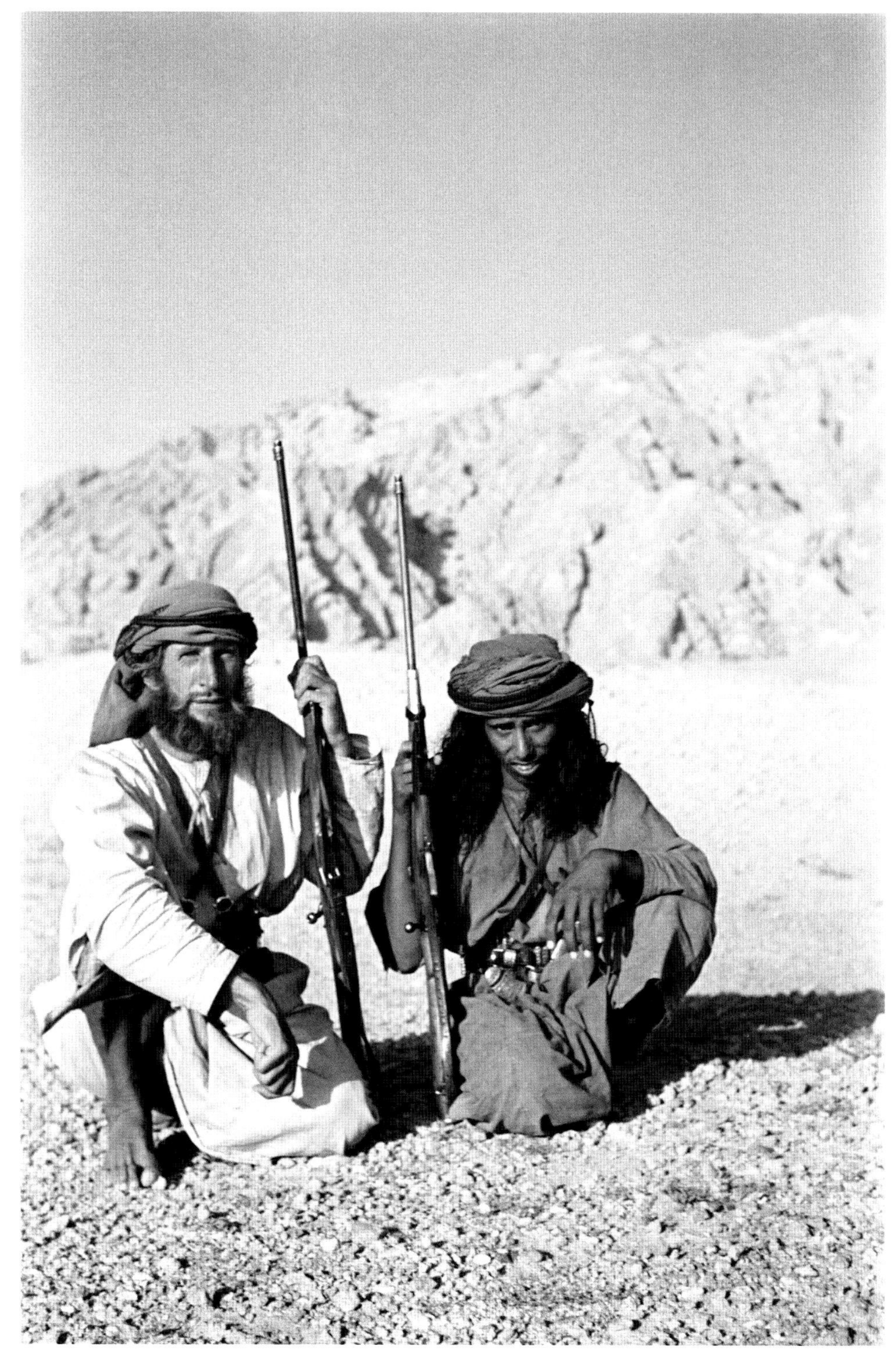

Wilfred Thesiger and
Salim bin Kabina, Abu Dhabi, 1949

CHARLES BUTT (1935–2006)

BORN INTO A MILITARY FAMILY in Surrey, England, in between the two World Wars, Charles Richard Butt was educated at Southey Hall in Bookham, where he developed a love of reading, and then at St. John's, in Leatherhead. After passing his exams at sixteen, he worked locally for a couple of years while waiting to join the British Army. In a memoir of his early schooling at Southey Hall, he wrote, "I cannot say that I enjoyed any of my schooldays anywhere—the best years of my life were with the British Army and several years with an Arabian force."

In 1953 Butt joined the Intelligence Corps and went to work in Field Security units in Germany, Belgium, Holland, Cyprus, Aden, and the Western Aden Protectorate. In 1960 Butt joined the reserves, known as the Territorial Army, while he investigated civilian life, notably spending four years working as a clerical officer for the Ministry of Defense. Meanwhile he returned to the Intelligence Corps as a photographic interpreter.

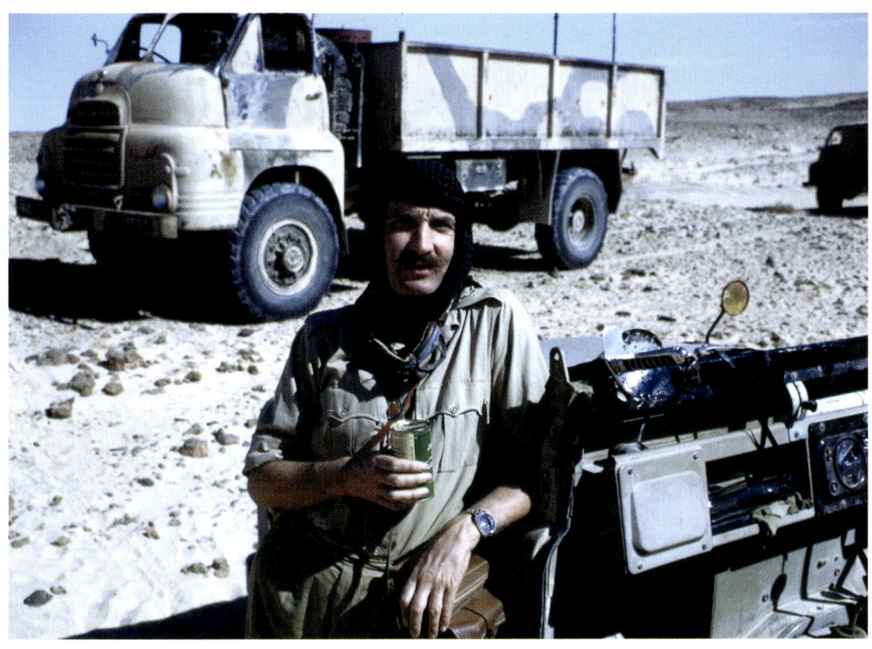

Captain Charlie Butt on an operation, Qathira, Dhofar, 1970

Butt decided to return to overseas service and in 1966 joined the Sultan of Oman's armed forces. A keen amateur photographer, Major Butt documented his twelve years in Oman with more than seven thousand 35 mm color slides, a diverse range of captioned images, ranging from military shots to landscapes, to photos of the inhabitants of Oman and intimate profiles of Sultan Qaboos.

After leaving the military in 1978, Butt continued to work in the Arab world, with administrative posts for international businesses in Algeria, Iraq, Sudan, and Saudi Arabia. He also took extensive photographs of Jordan and Saudi Arabia in the early 1980s. In 1989, in his fifties, he moved to Tydd St. Mary, in Lincolnshire, to take over and run the Five Bells Inn, a village pub.

With interests in travel, history, and writing in addition to photography, Butt was a member of the Royal Photographic Society, the Royal Geographical Society, and the Anglo-Arab Association. His photographs were bequeathed to the Middle East Centre Archive at St. Antony's College, Oxford University, in 2007.

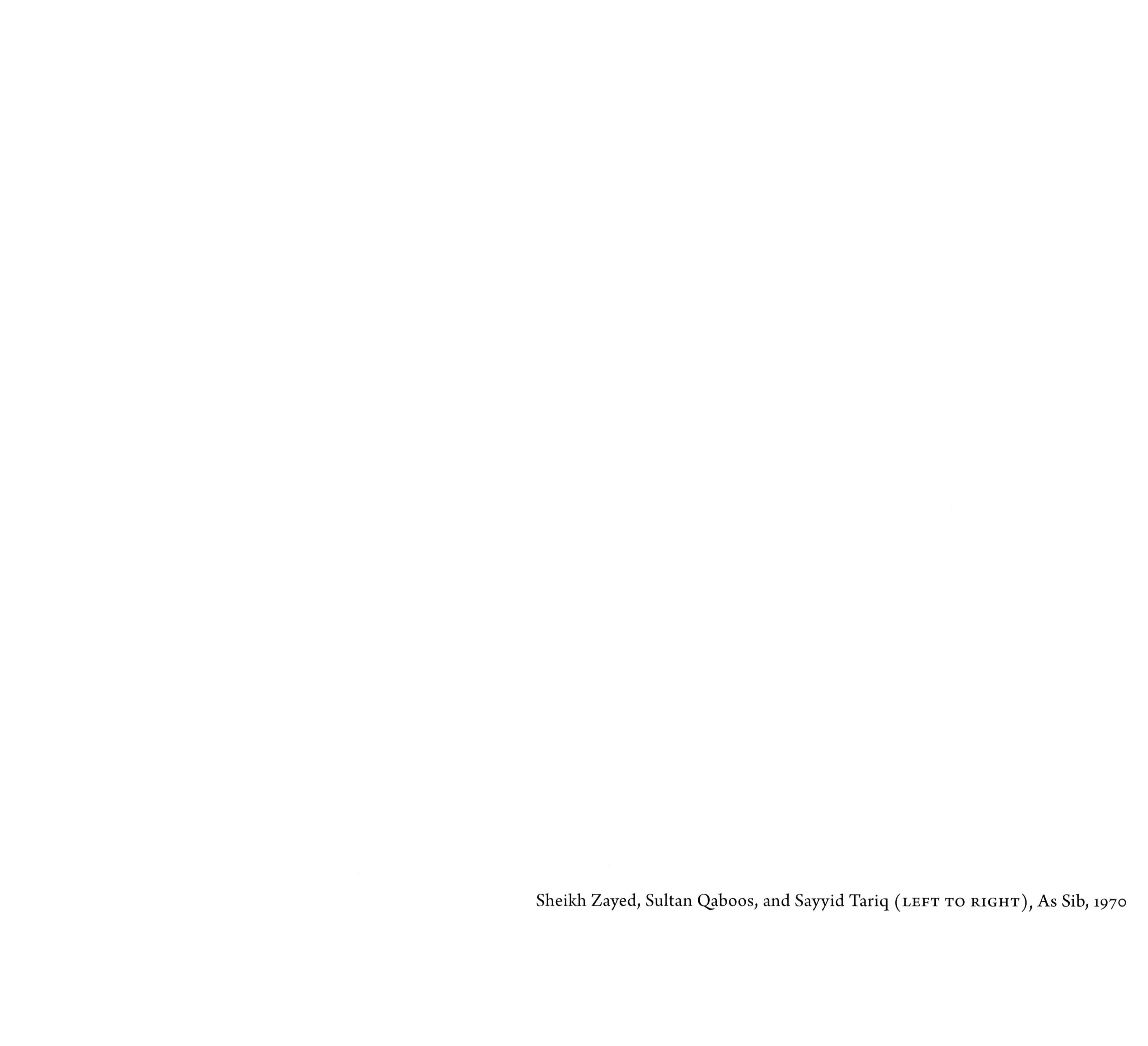

Sheikh Zayed, Sultan Qaboos, and Sayyid Tariq (LEFT TO RIGHT), As Sib, 1970

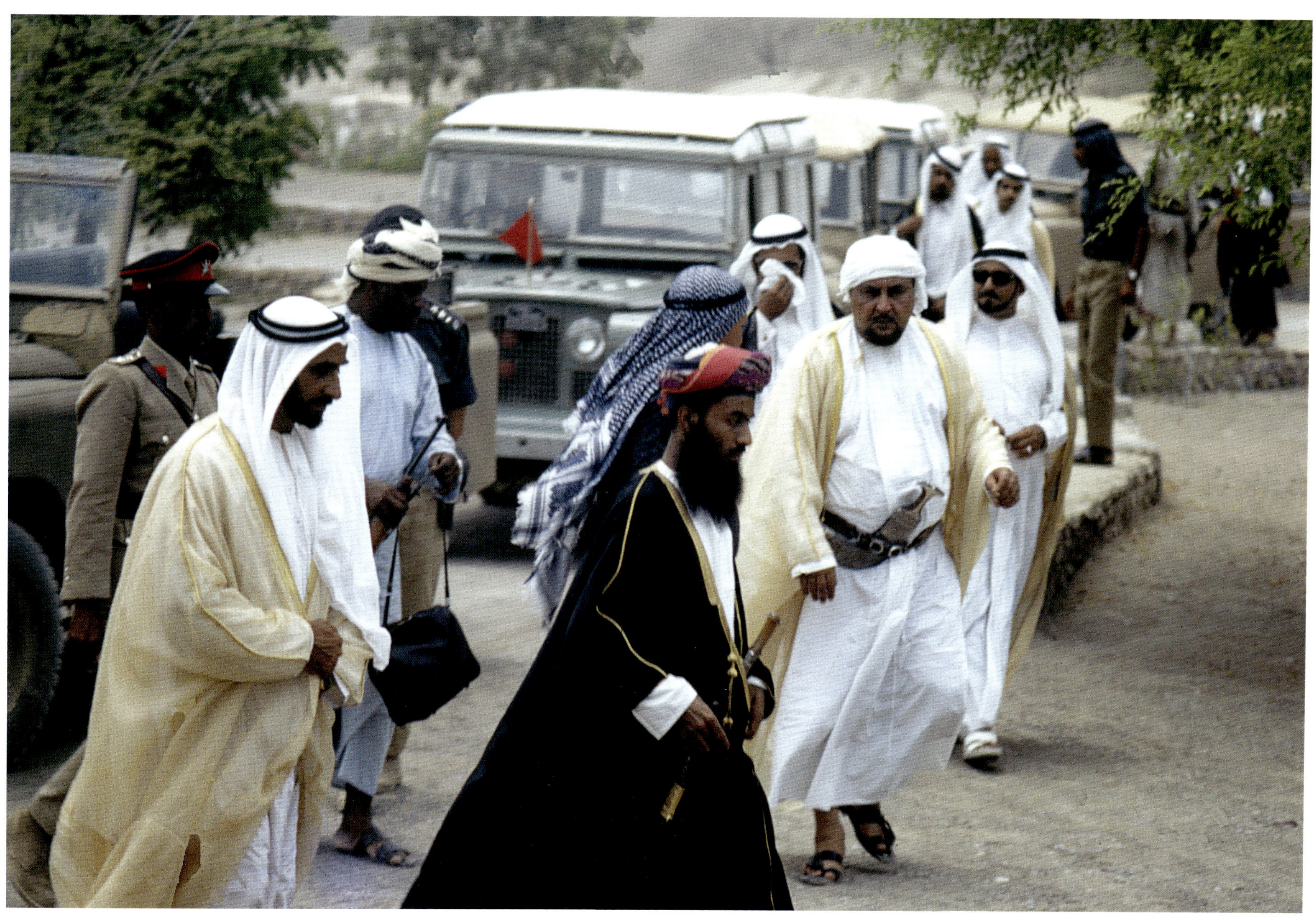

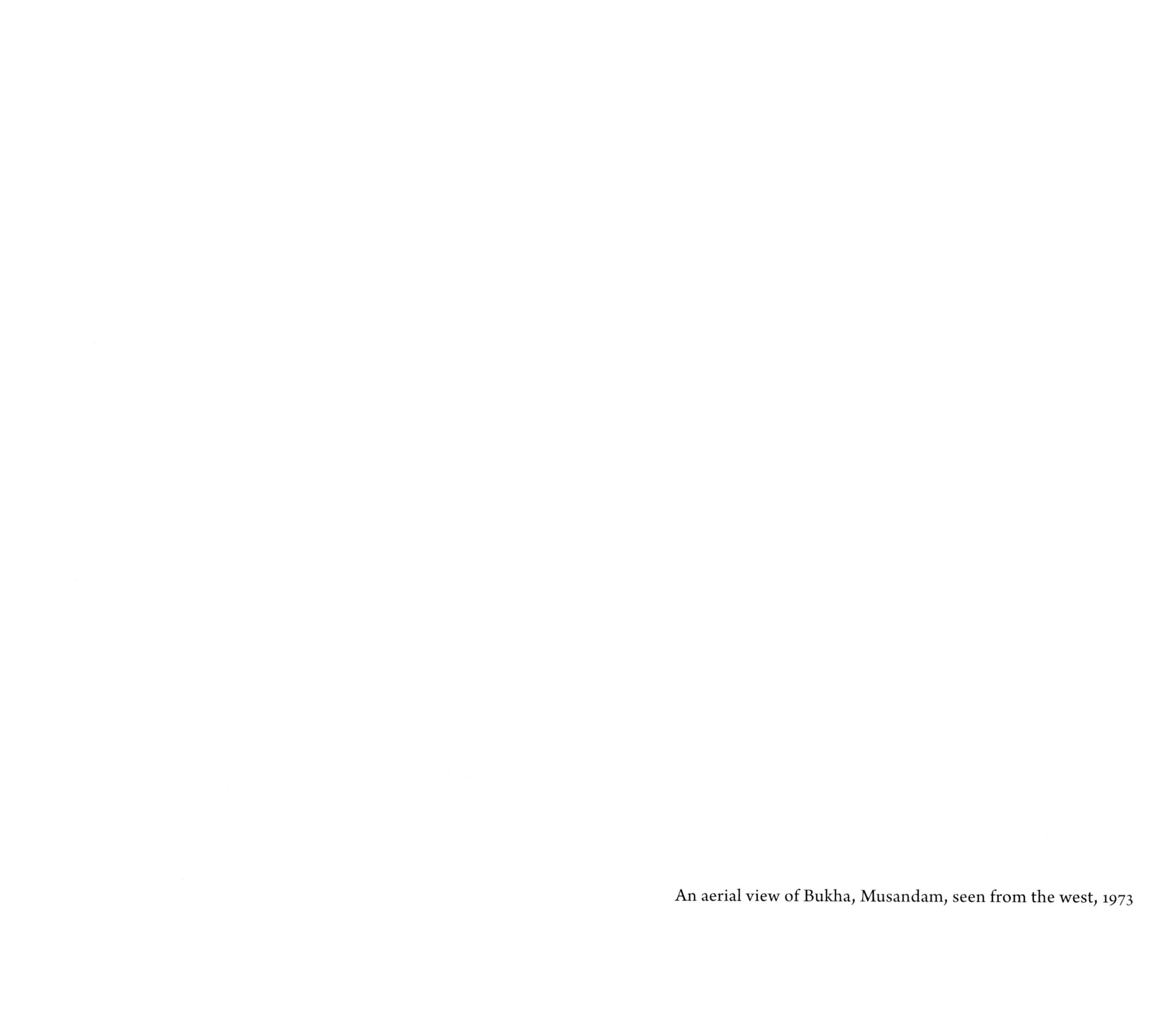

An aerial view of Bukha, Musandam, seen from the west, 1973

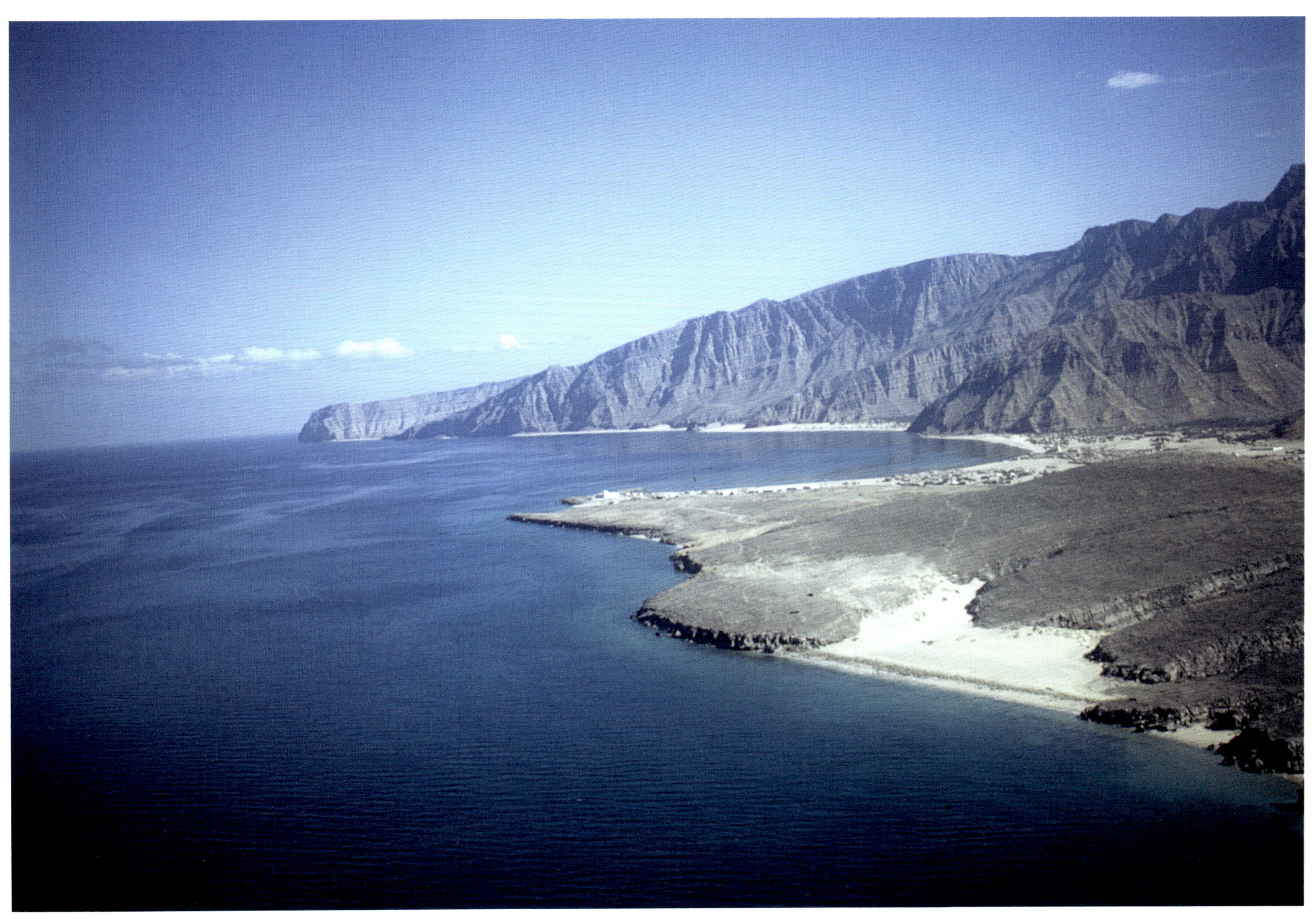

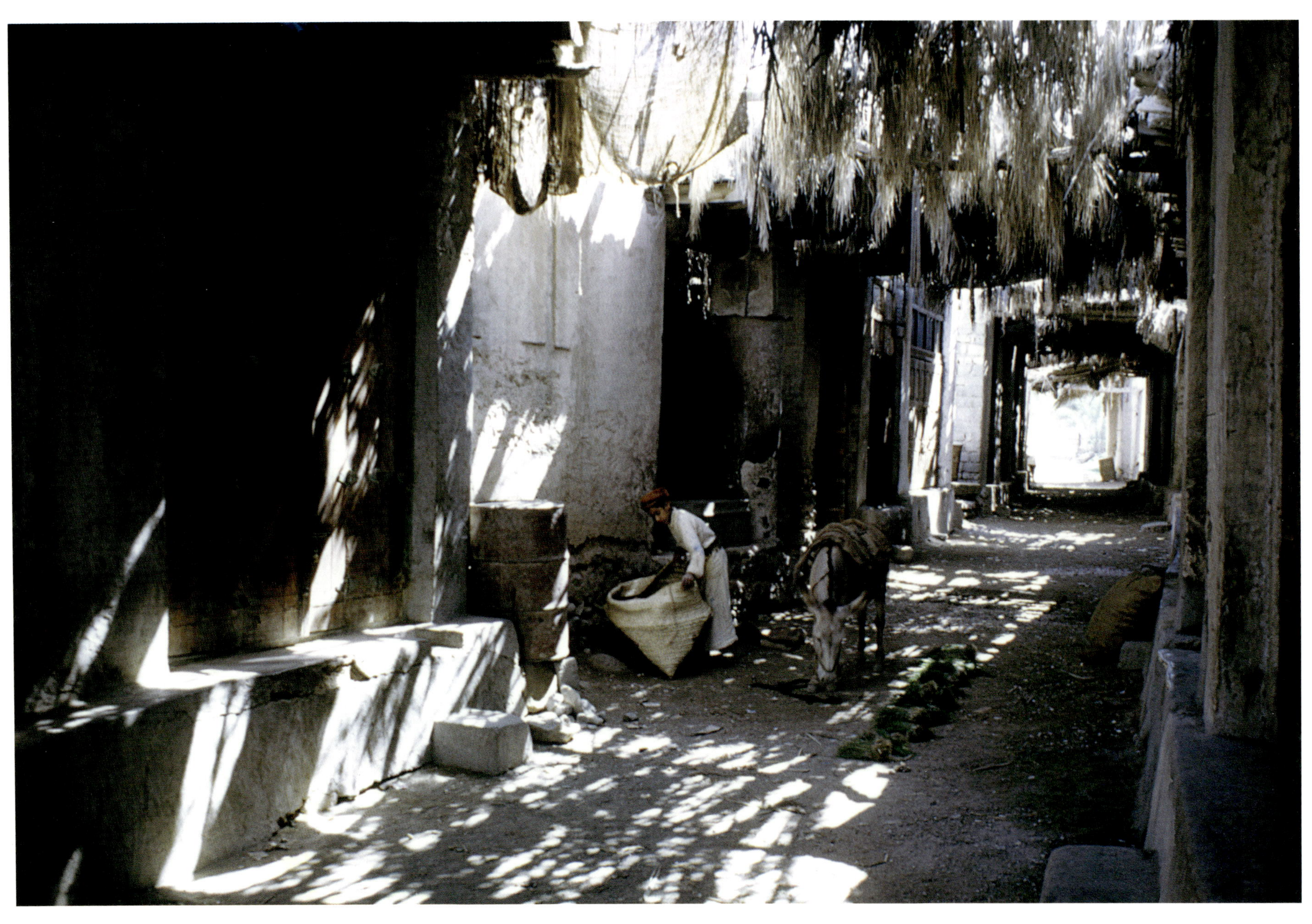

Souk during midday siesta, Nakhal, 1969

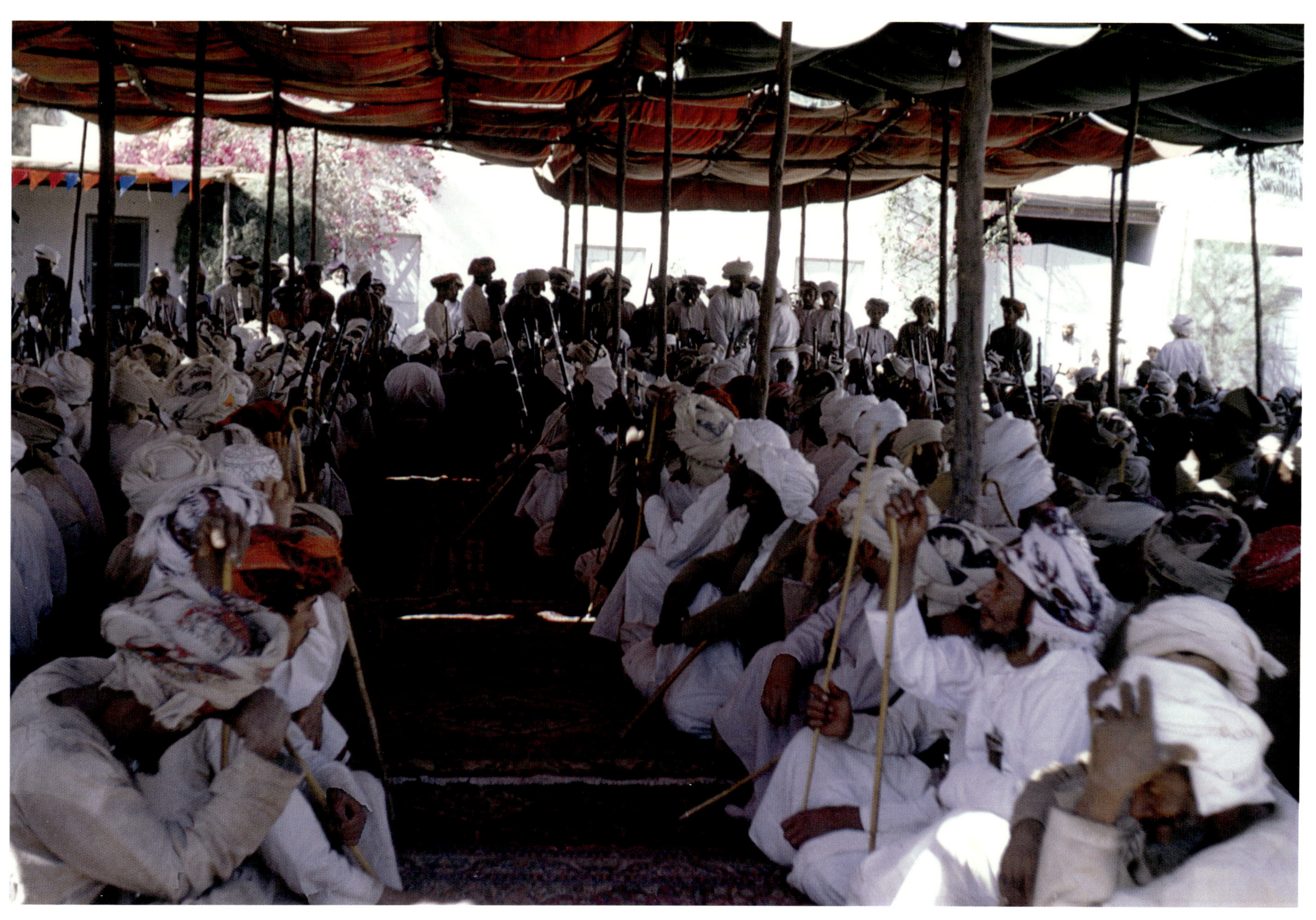

Farmer's day, men awaiting speechmaking, Nizwa, 1967

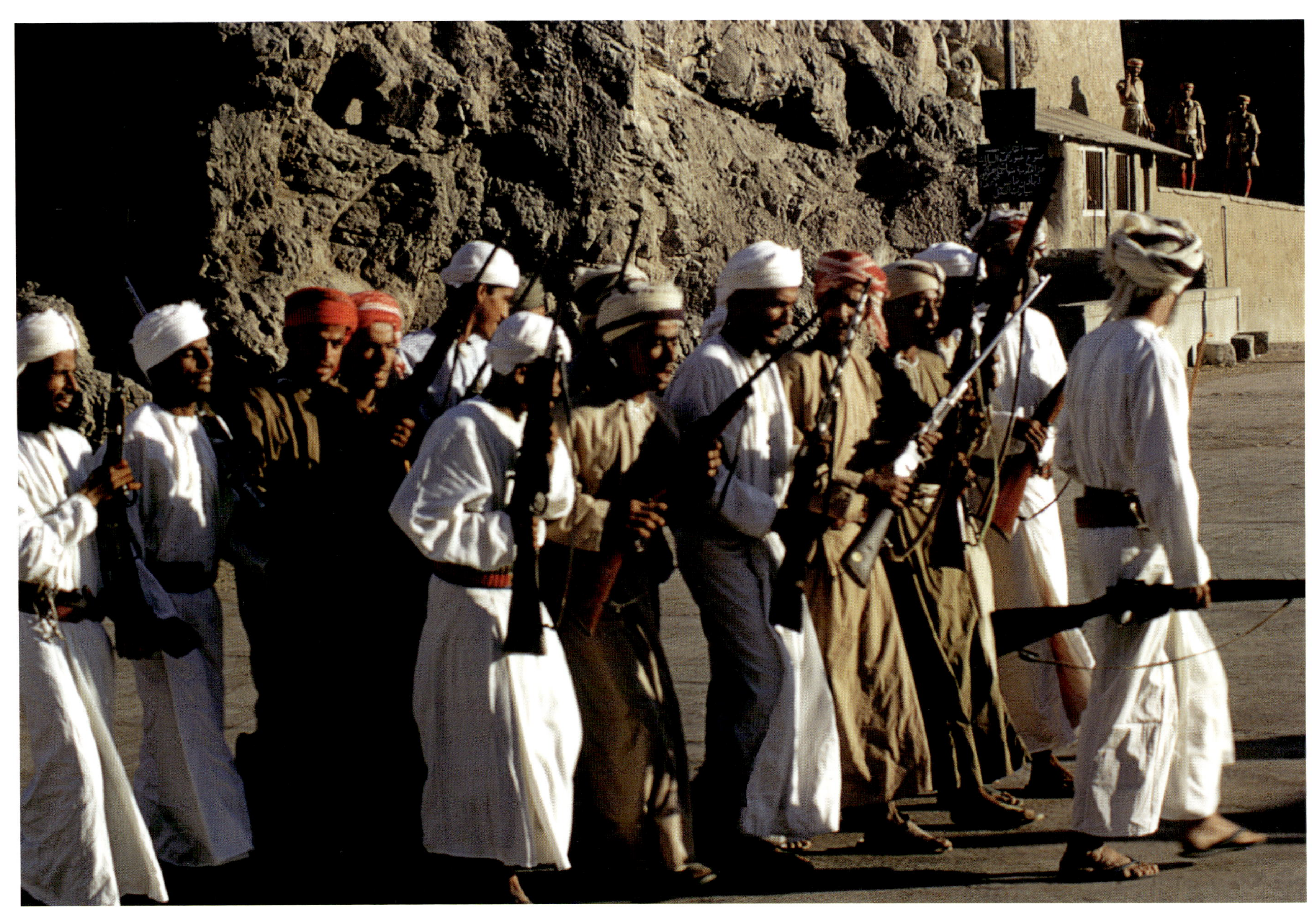

Singing after bringing up rear of Eid al-Fitr procession along the mall after prayers, Muscat, 1969

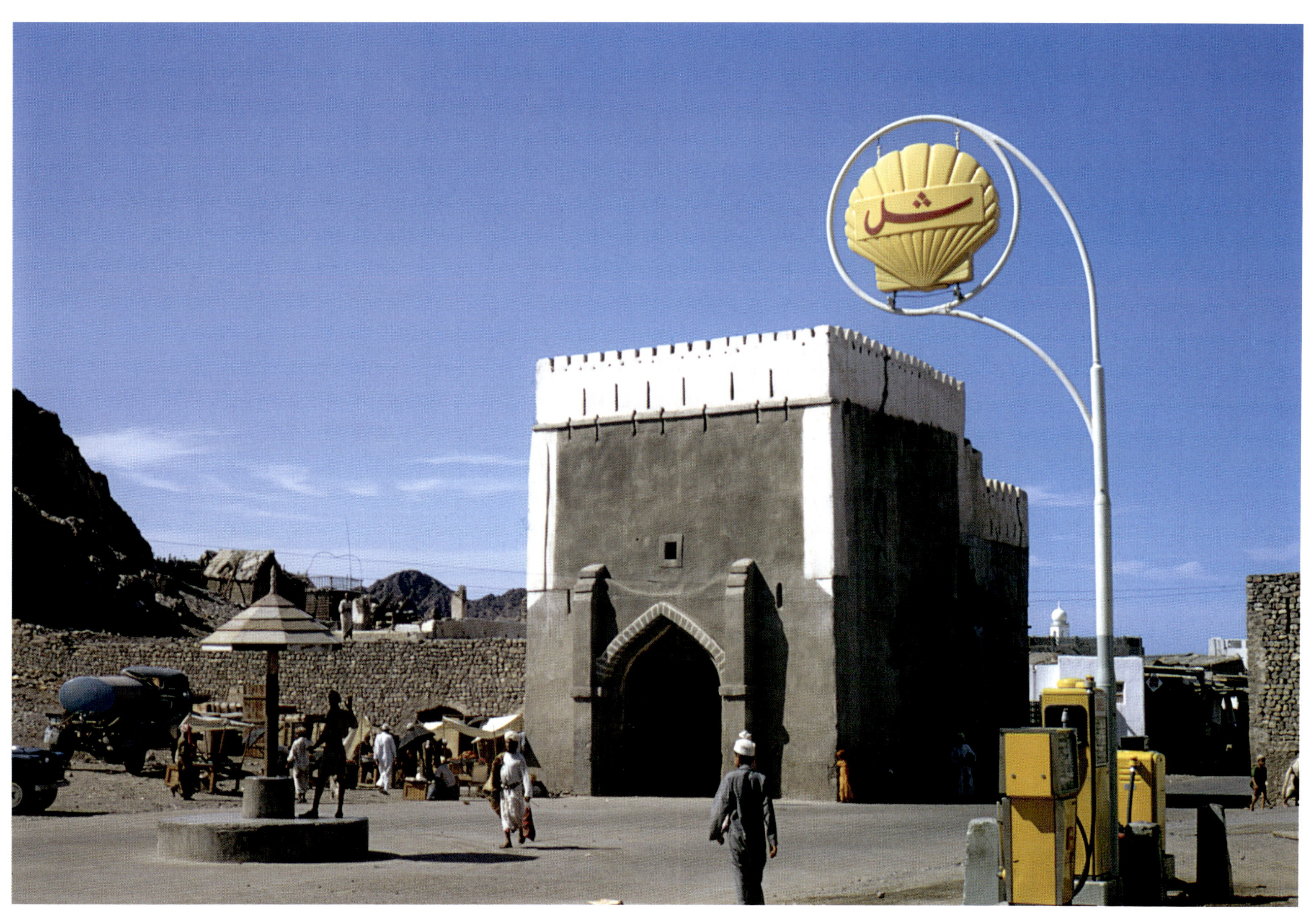

Main gate, Muttrah, 1967

Mango boats, Muscat, 1970

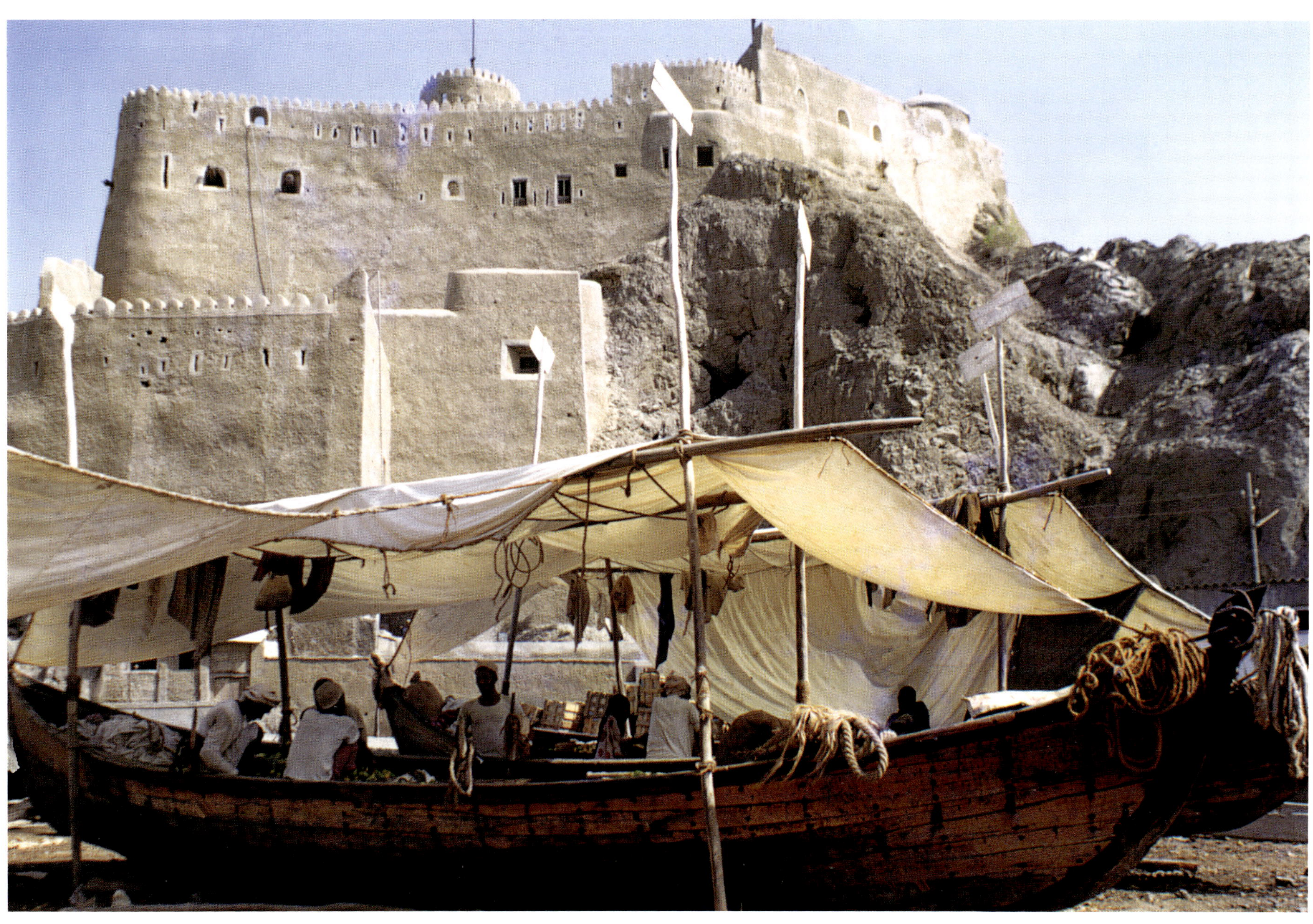

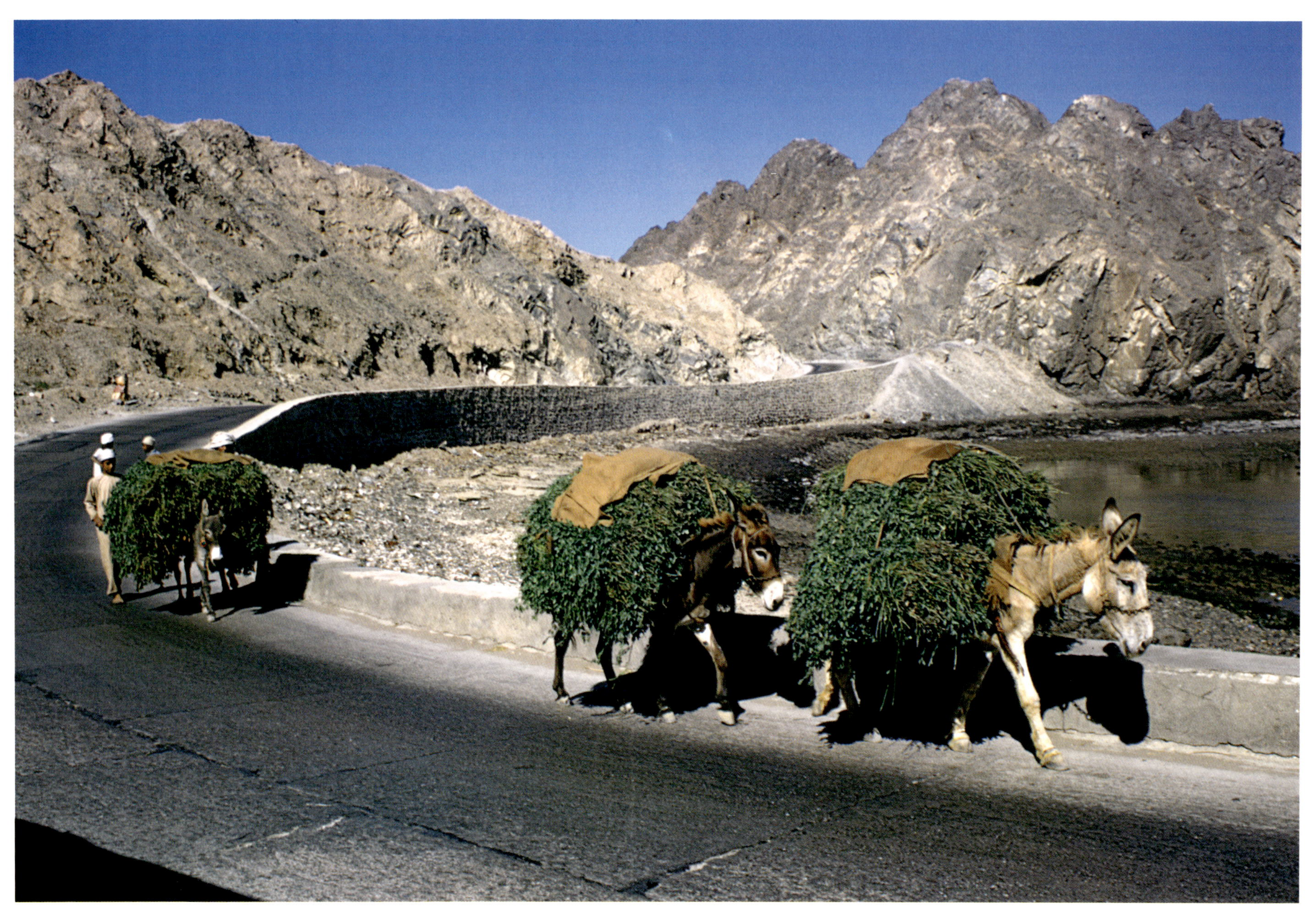

Donkeys carrying fodder (alfalfa) on the coastal road by Riyam Bay, Muscat, 1969

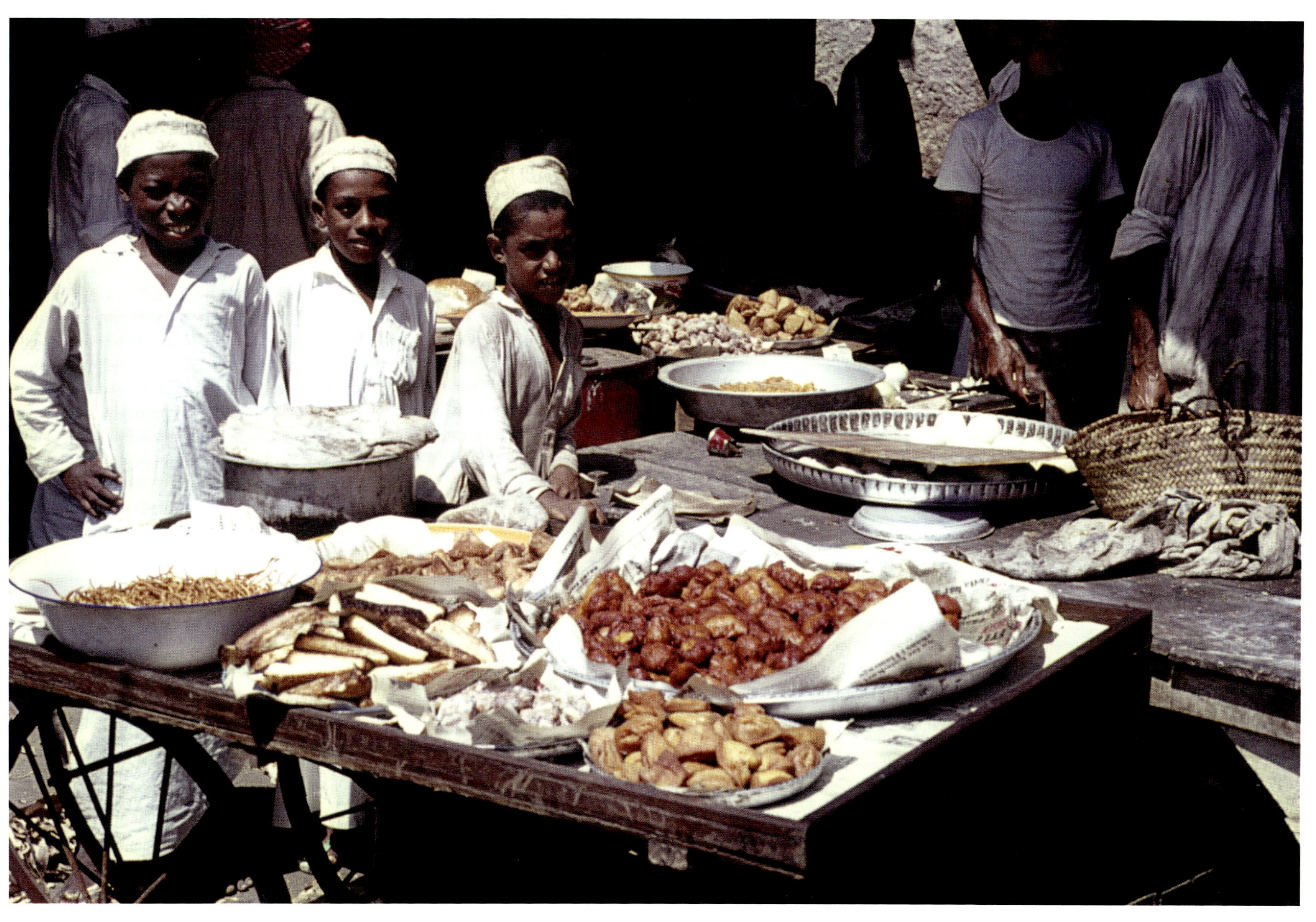

Boys selling *tastiet* in the souk, Muttrah, 1967

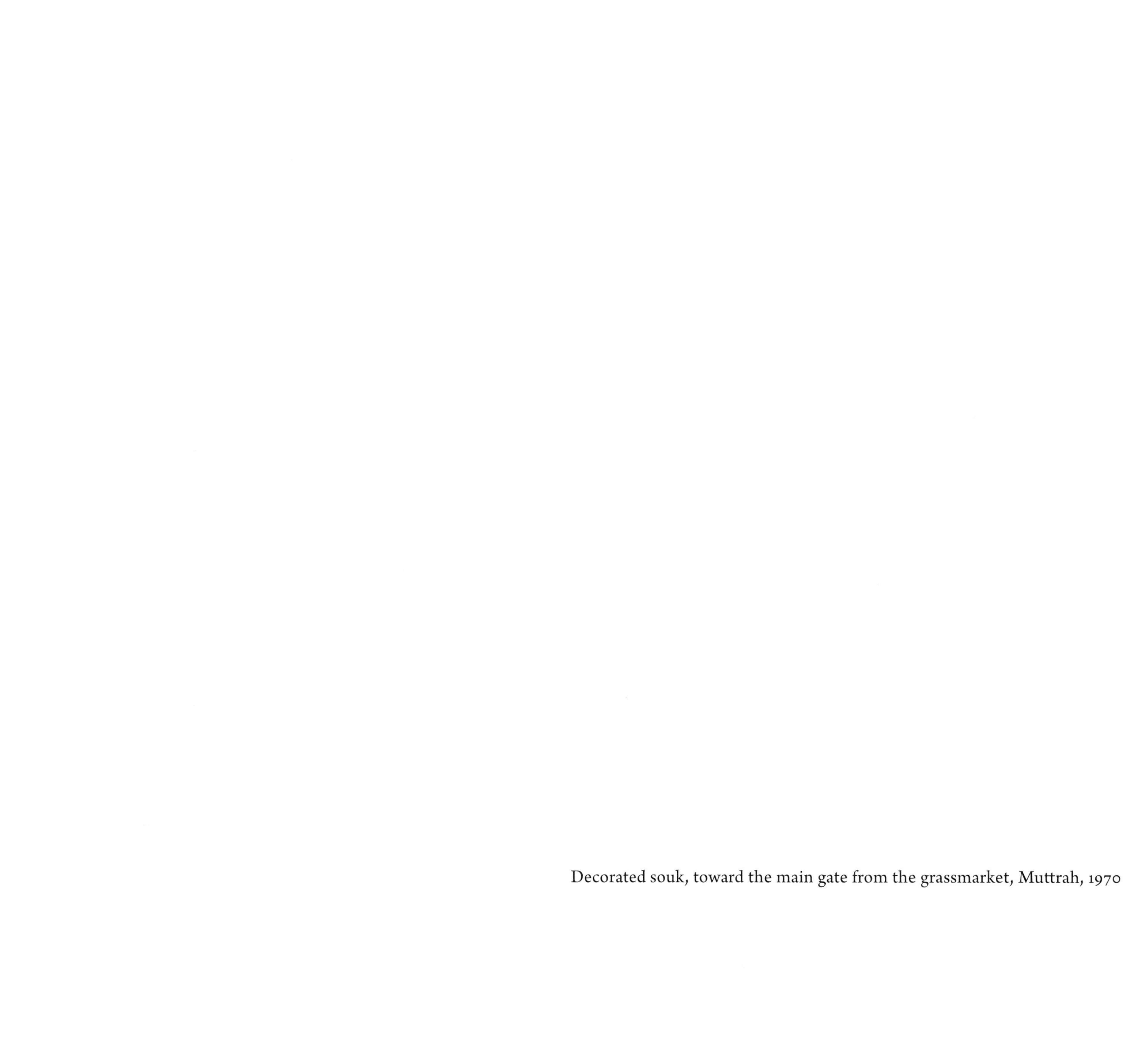

Decorated souk, toward the main gate from the grassmarket, Muttrah, 1970

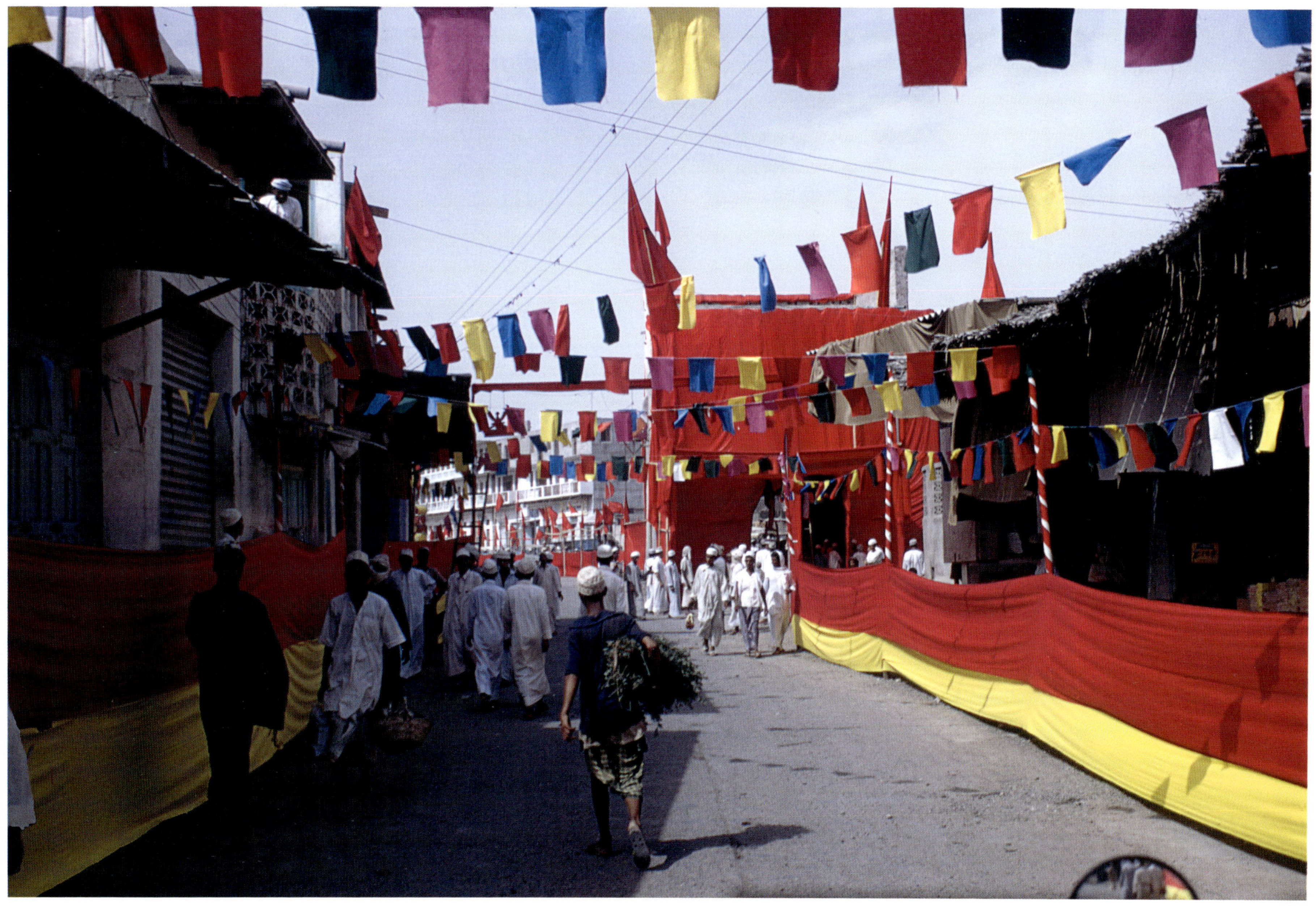

Young wife from the
Shihu tribe, Harf, 1973

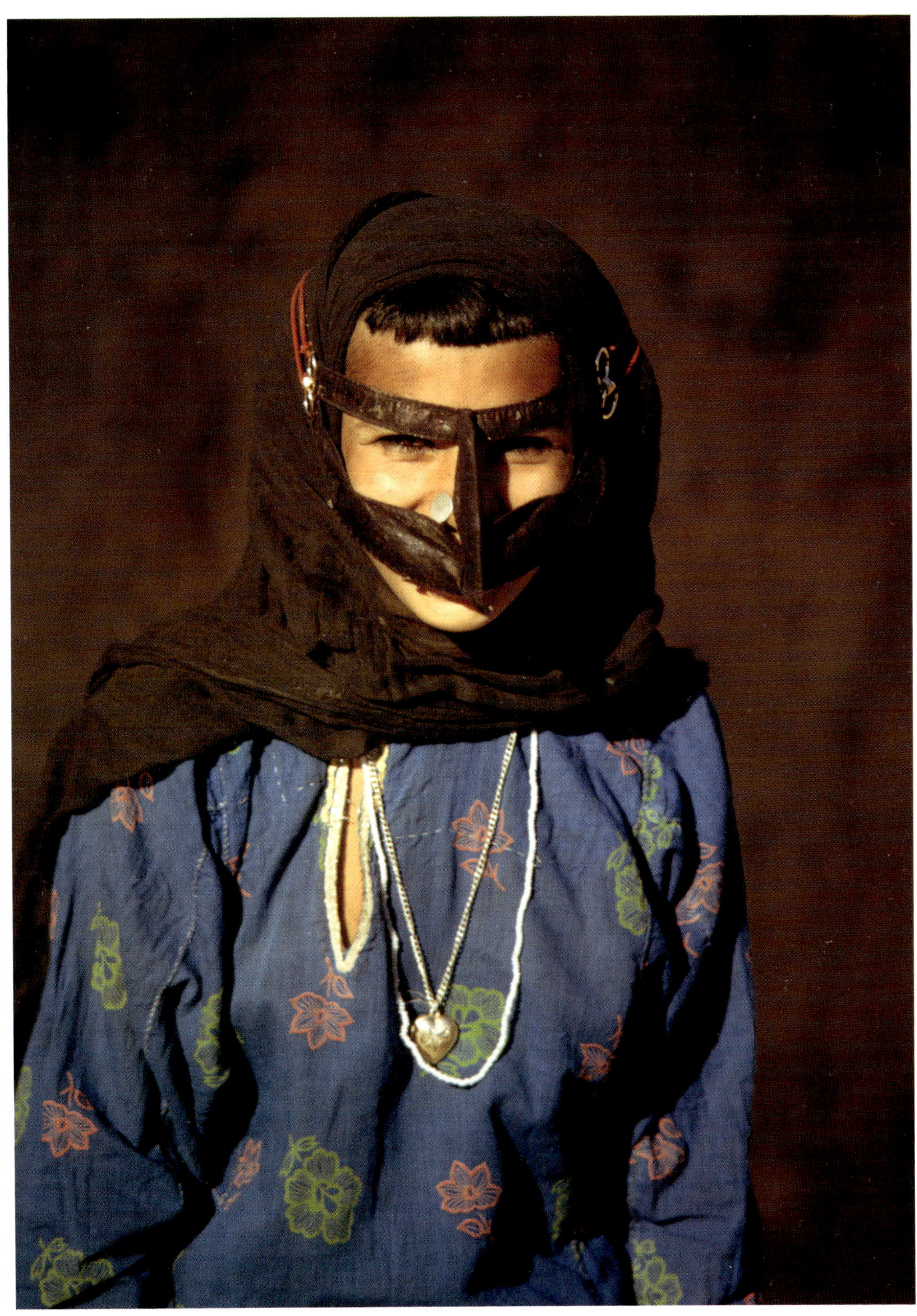

H.M. Sultan Qaboos bin Said al-Said,
Sultan of Oman, Dhofar, 1975

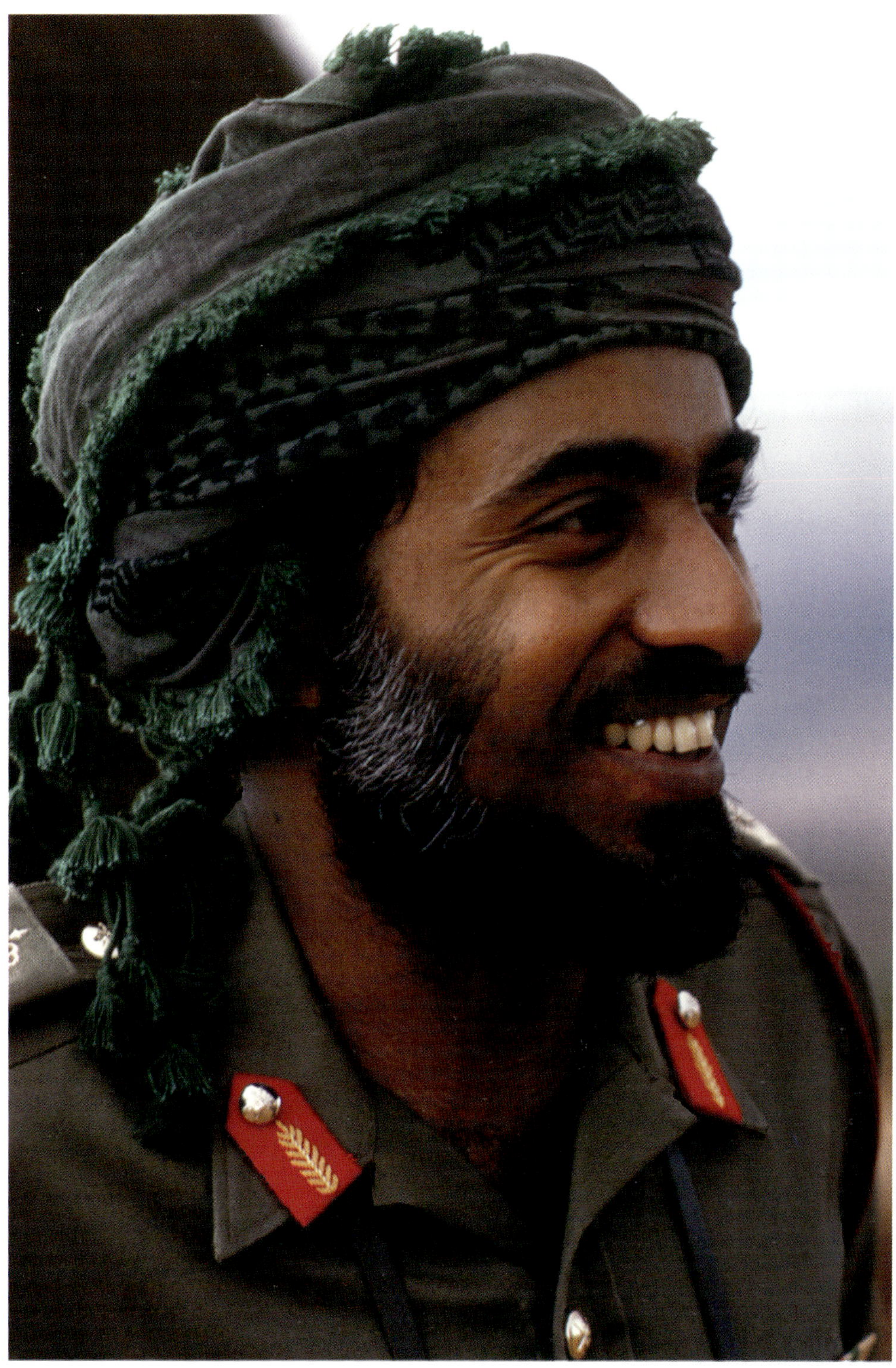

Threshing, Wadi Bani Kharous, Masirah, 1971

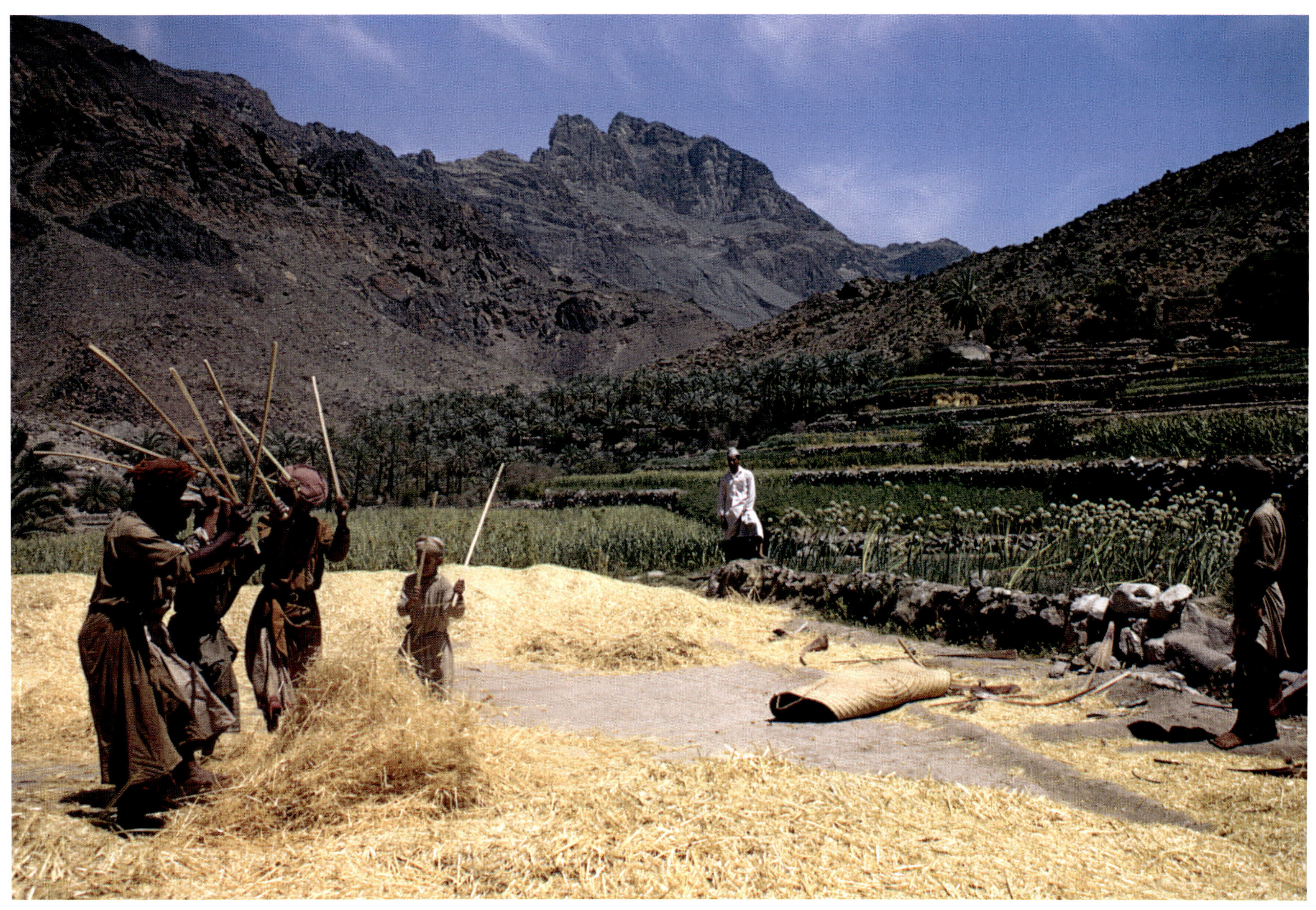

Village gate, Wishal, 1971

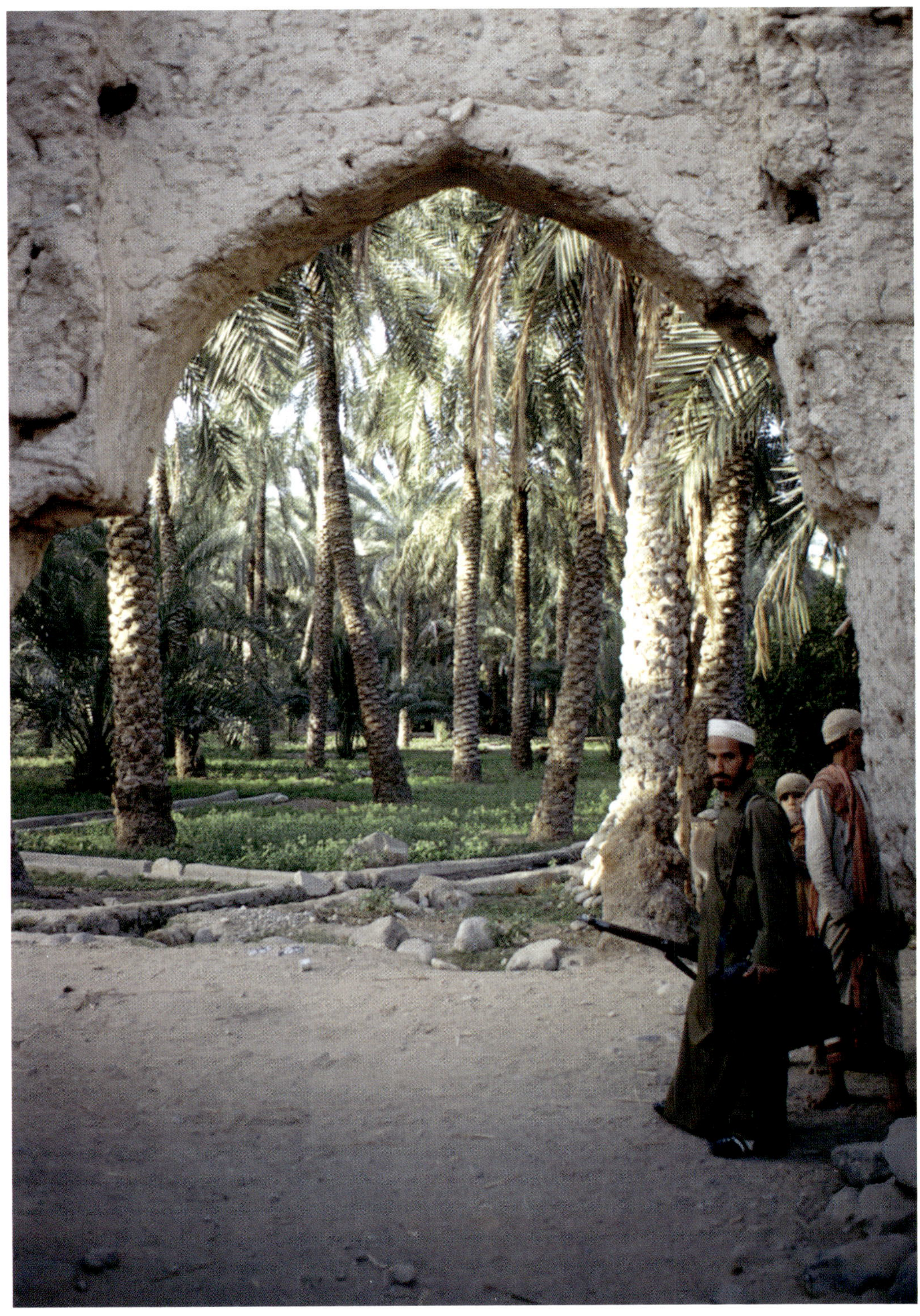

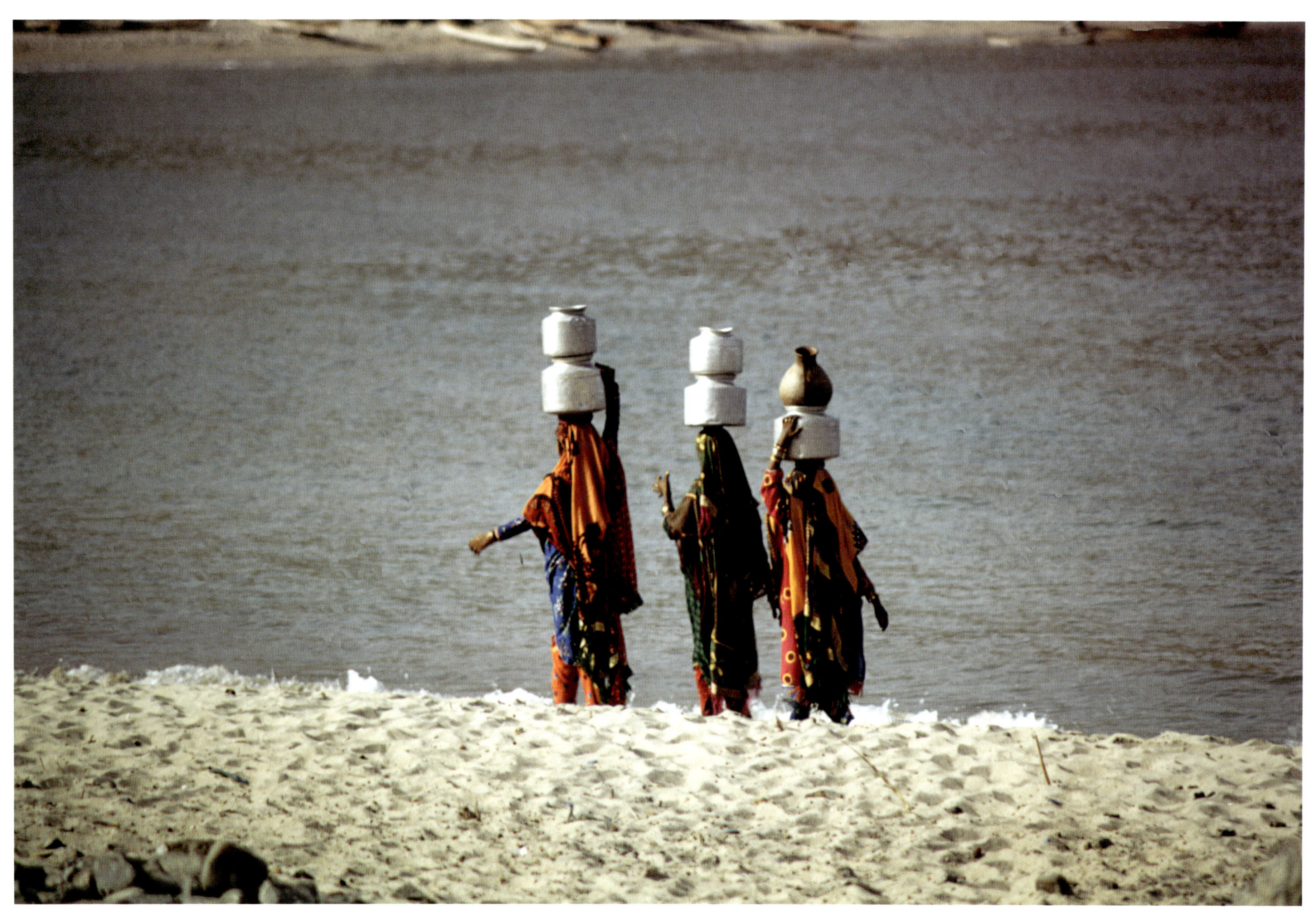

Baluch fisherwomen going to a village well, Sidab, 1970

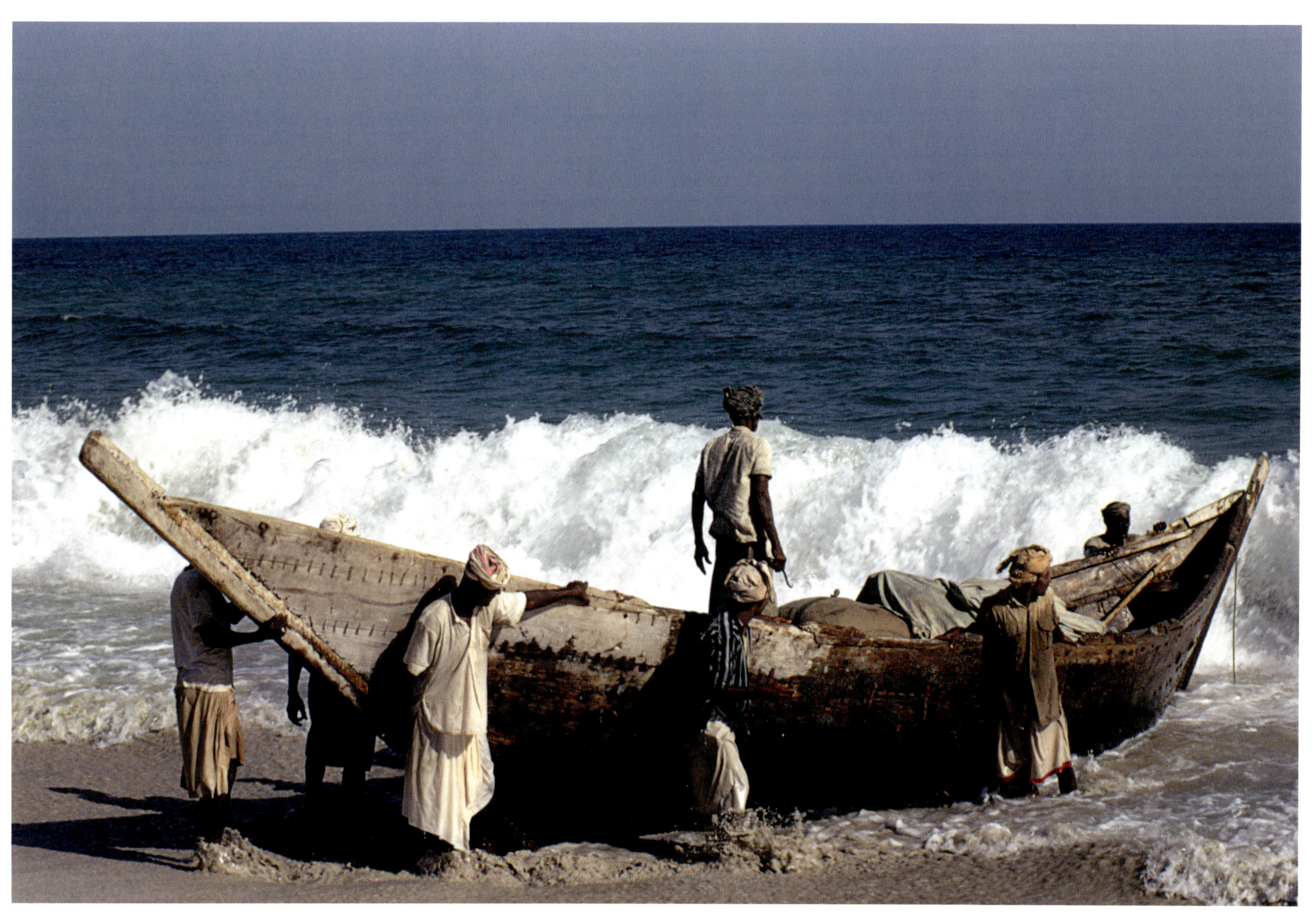

Beaching a cargo ferry, Salalah, 1969

Main Street, Hamra, 1976

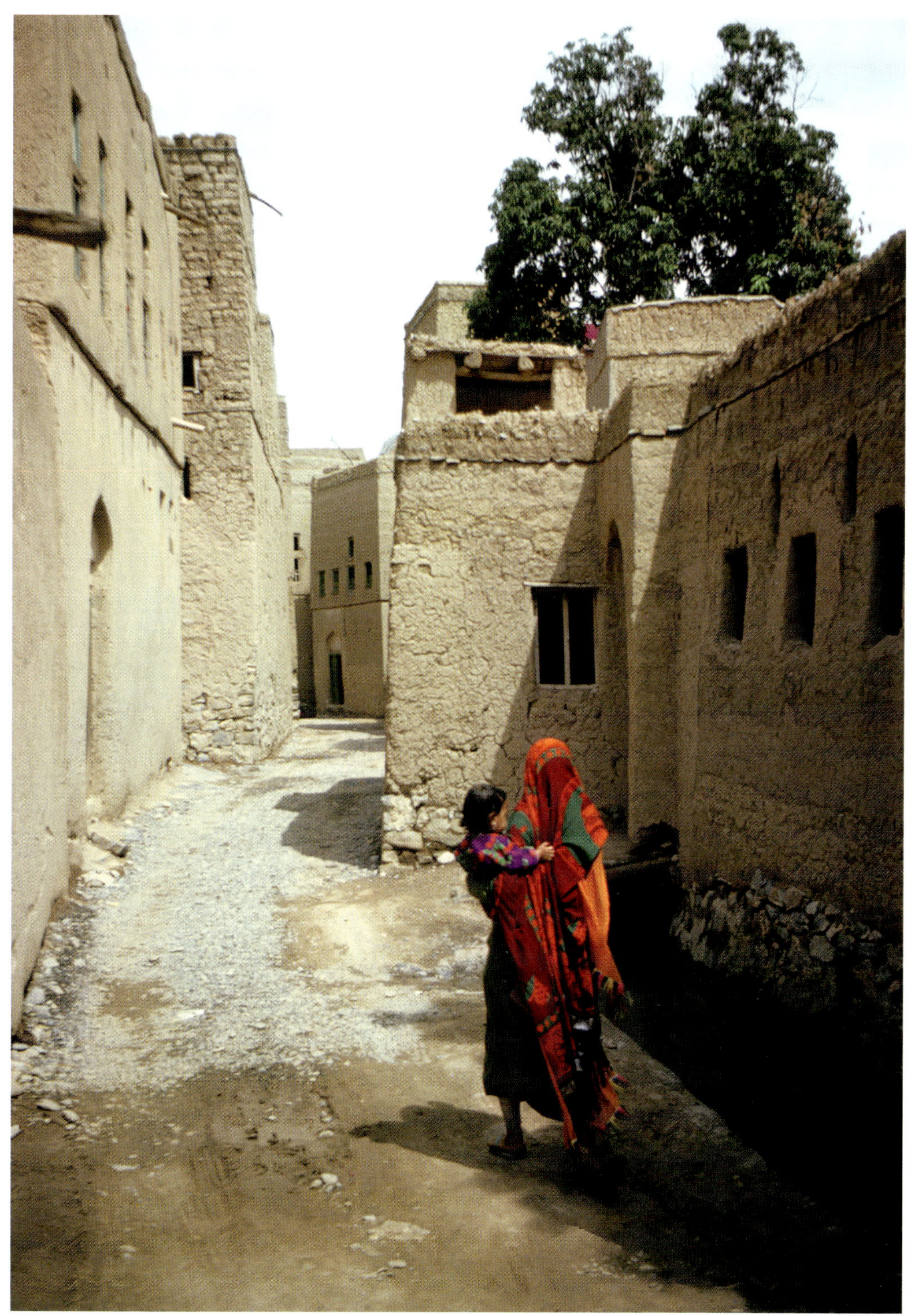

Mango boat, Muscat, 1970

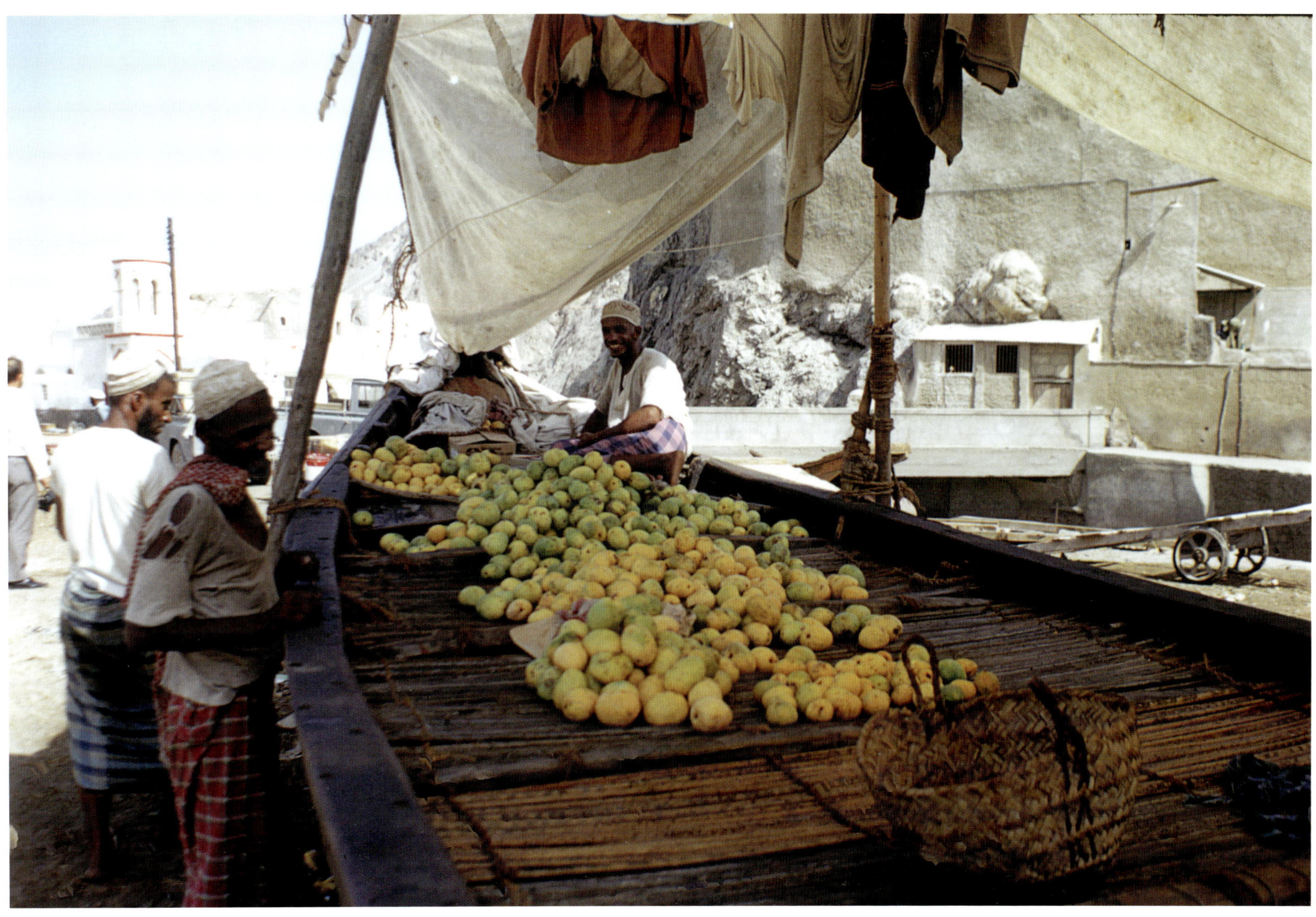

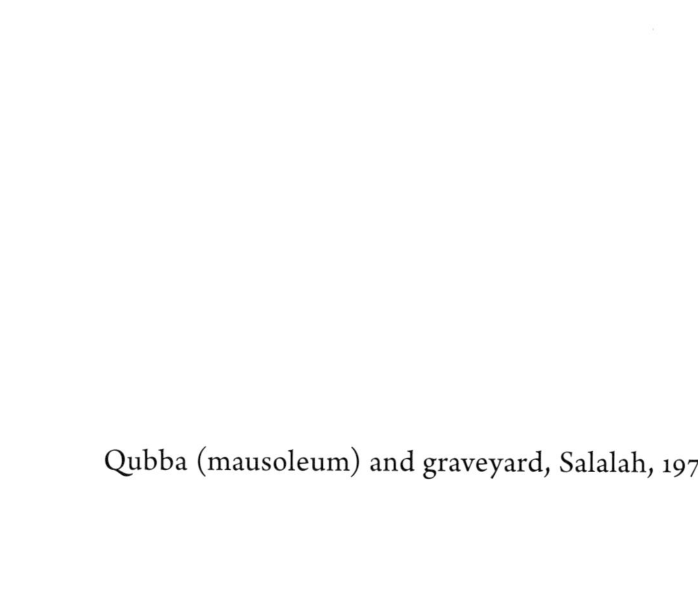

Qubba (mausoleum) and graveyard, Salalah, 1973

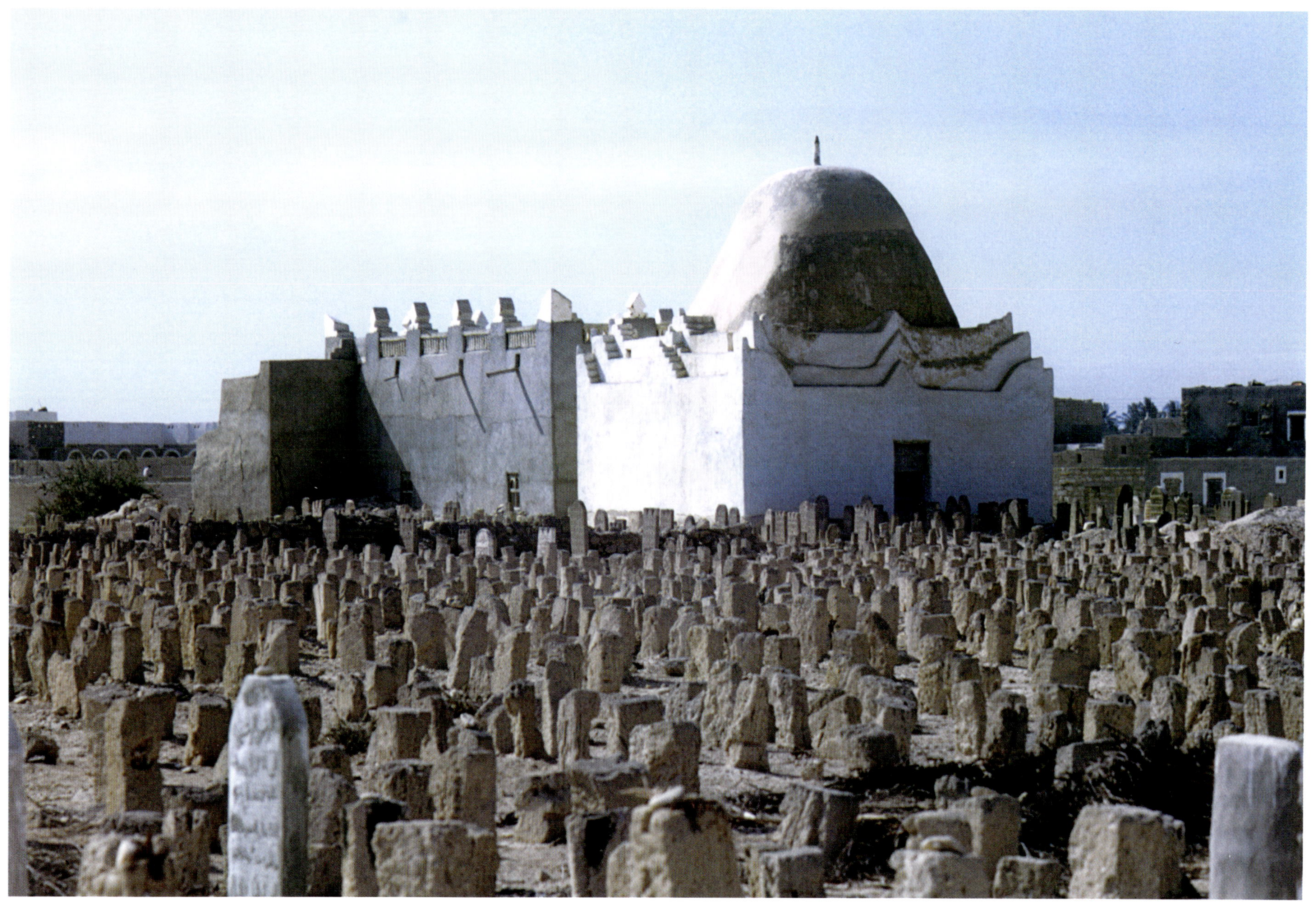

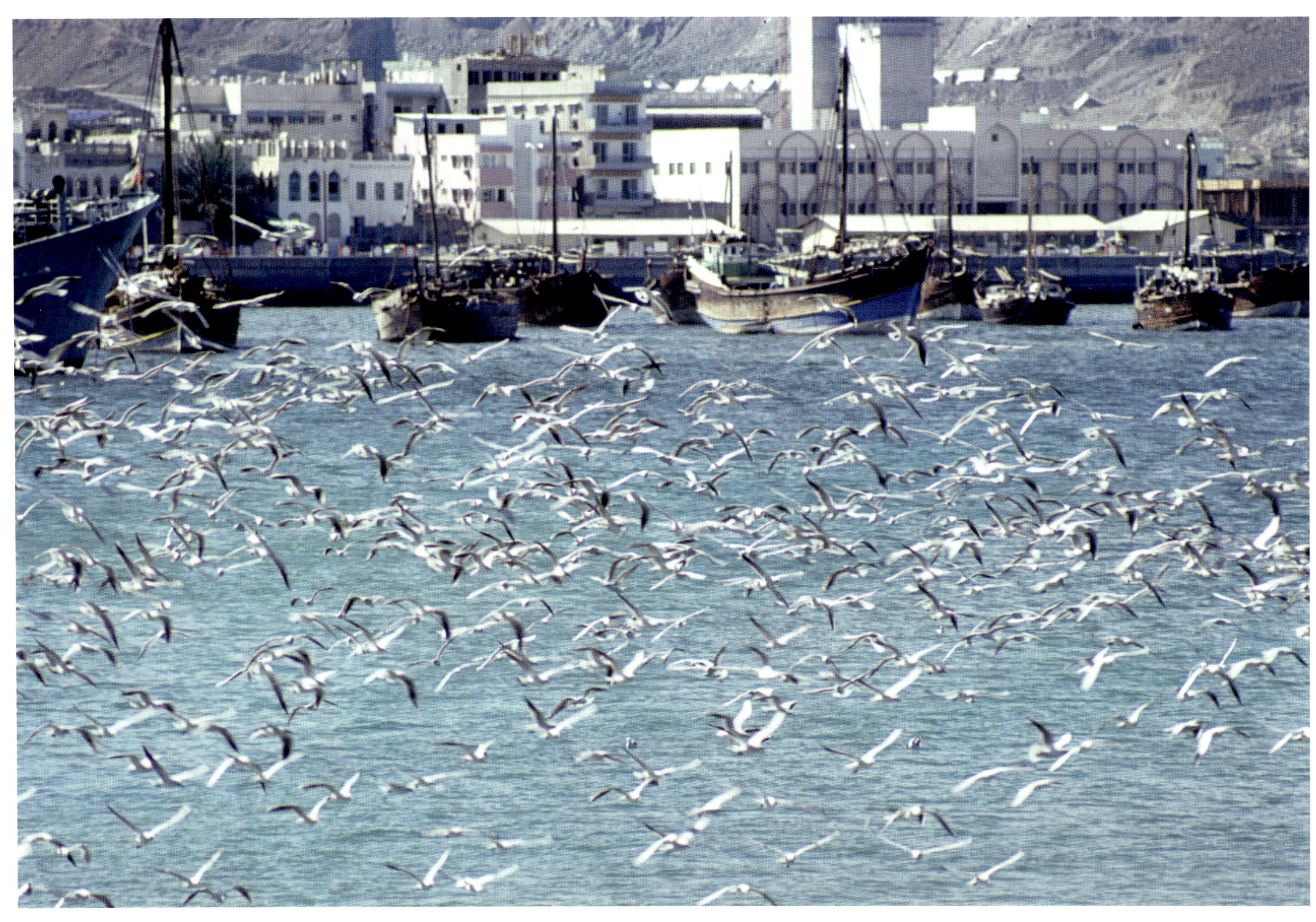

Massed seabirds, Mina Qaboos, Muttrah, 1976

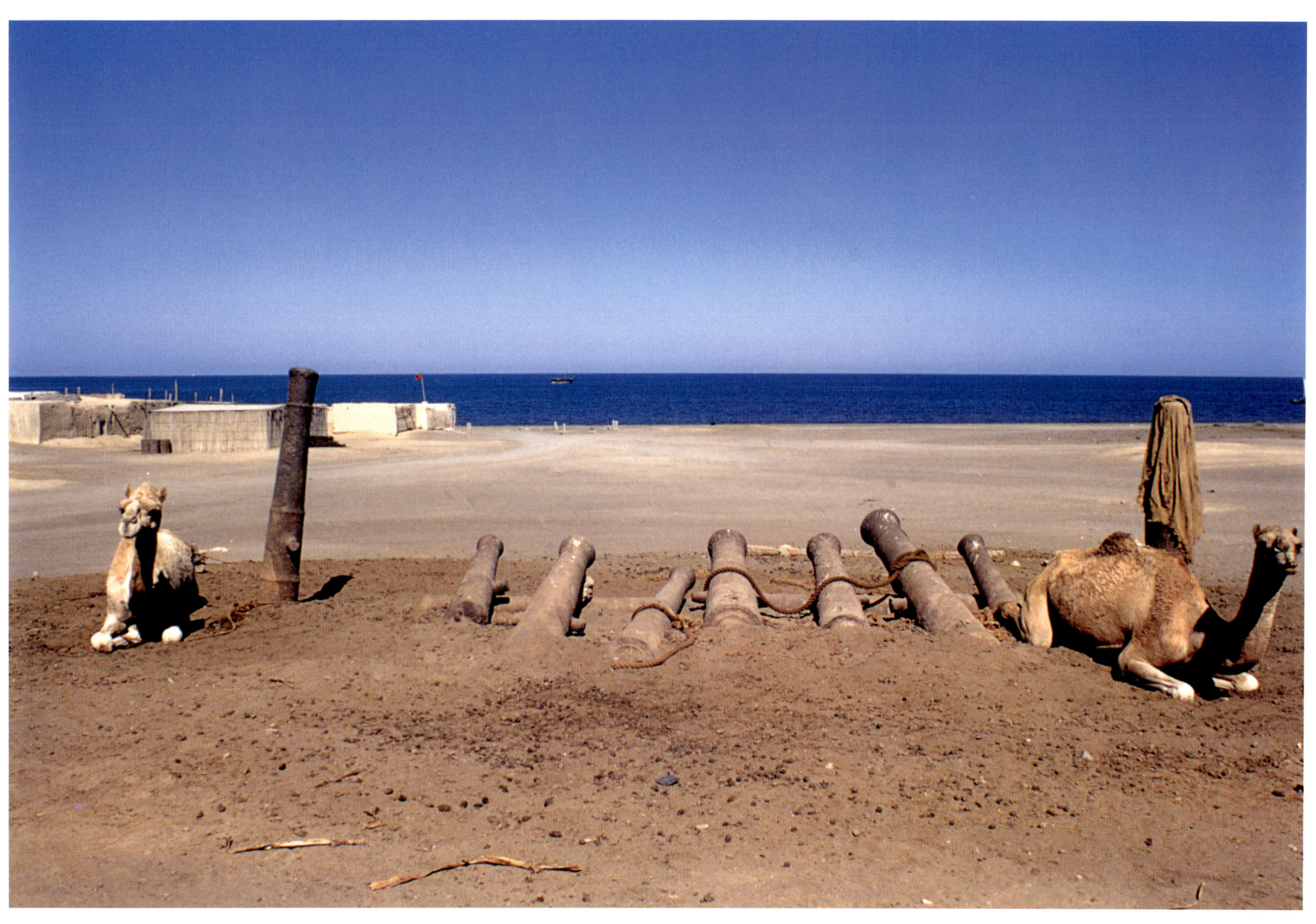

The Wali's saluting battery, Suwaiq, 1970

Detail of purple dye pots (made only at Bahlah), Firq, 1969

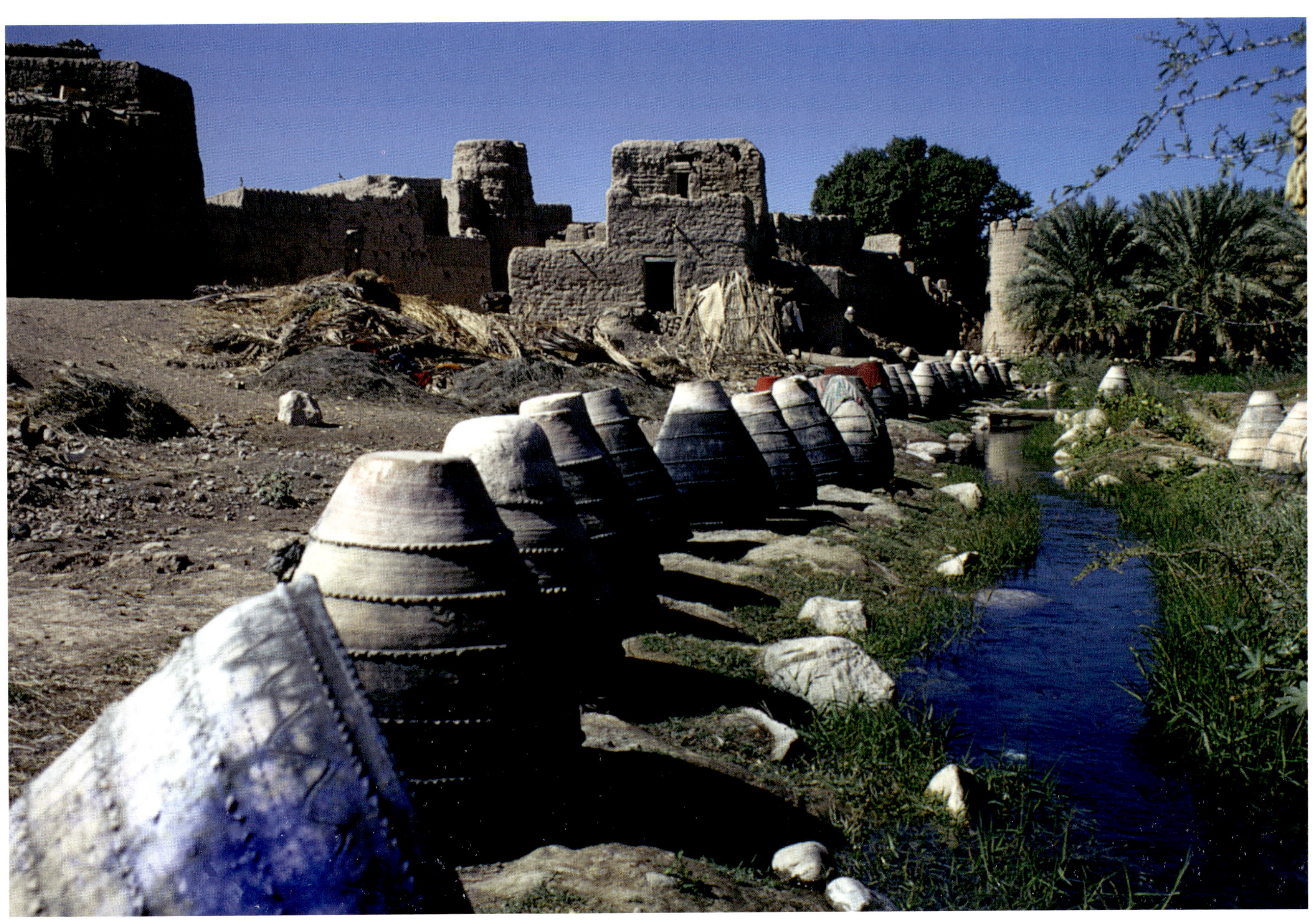

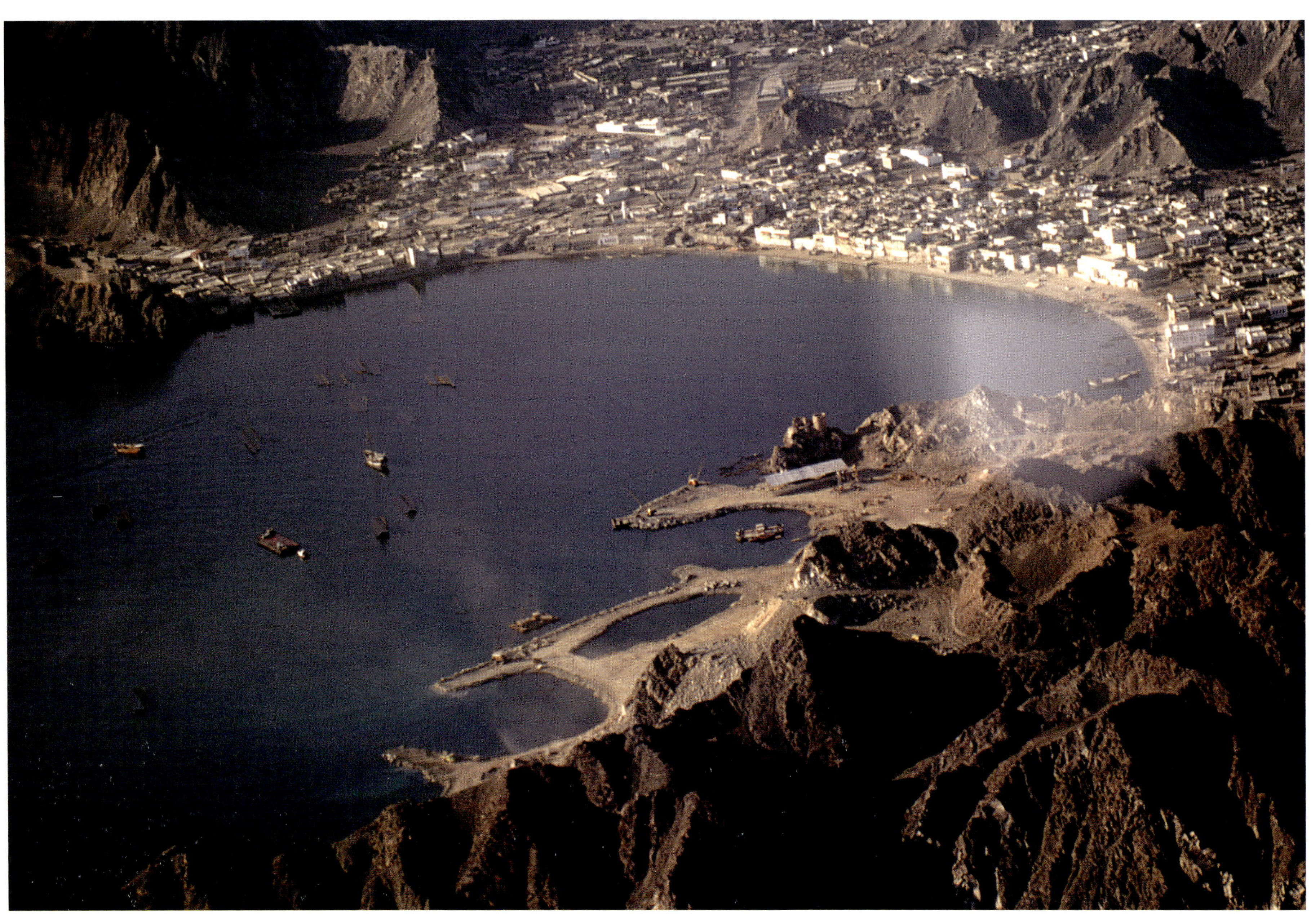

Muttrah from the air, 1970

EDWARD GRAZDA (born in 1947)

NEW YORK CITY NATIVE, Ed Grazda grew up in Flushing, Queens, and started taking pictures in high school. After graduating with a BFA in photography from the Rhode Island School of Design, he went to Mexico in 1972, attracted to the cultural variety and richness of Latin American cultures. For the next seven years, he spent several months a year exploring and photographing daily life in Central and South America, shooting not only in Mexico but also in Guatemala, Peru, Ecuador, and Bolivia. Fifty vintage silver gelatin prints of Grazda's photos from this period were exhibited in a 2008 show at the Sepia Gallery called "Recuerdo: A Memory of Latin America 1972–1979." Reviewing the exhibition in the *New Yorker,* critic Vince Aletti wrote that Grazda's work "may remind viewers of Henri Cartier-Bresson, Robert Frank and other keen observers of people in public" and "delivers an understated kind of amazement."

By 1980, Grazda's attention was turning to Asia, where the social and cultural change he was interested in shooting was happening much more quickly. His travels took him through Hong Kong, China, Thailand, Burma, and India. While in Delhi, just after the Soviet Union invaded Afghanistan, Grazda met some young Afghan refugees. This chance meeting led him to Peshawar and then to the Pakistan-Afghan border—the beginning of a twenty-five-year relationship with Afghanistan that has documented the impact of decades of war on the Afghan people. The substantial work he did in Pakistan and Afghanistan led to the publication of two monographs: *Afghanistan 1980–1989* (Der Alltag, 1990) and *Afghanistan Diary 1992–2000* (PowerHouse Books, 2000).

The photographs of Oman in this volume were commissioned in 2005 by the Islam-West Engagement Project, a multifaceted initiative jointly developed by the Institute for American Values, in New York City, and the Ministry of Awqaf and Religious Affairs, in Oman. To create an intimate portrait of contemporary Oman, Grazda spent three months traveling throughout the country, capturing moments

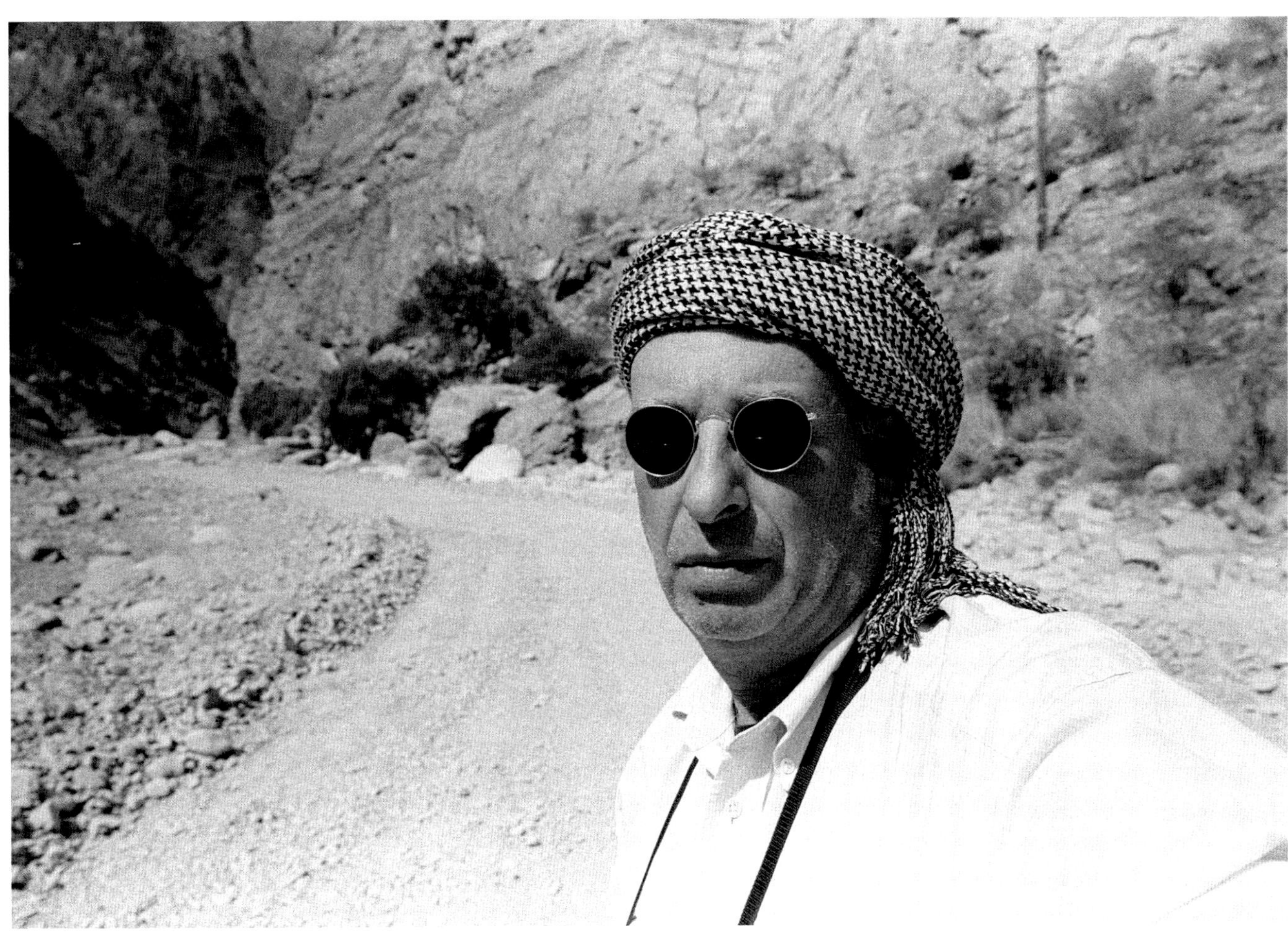

Edward Grazda in Oman, 2005

of daily life. Grazda used—as he always has—a 35 mm Leica, which he describes as small, unobtrusive, and simply "the best camera there is." Raina Sacks Blankenhorn and Abdulrahman al-Salimi selected two hundred of the resulting images to display as silver gelatin prints in the first large-scale photography exhibition held in Muscat.

Grazda's work has been collected by New York City's Metropolitan Museum of Art and Museum of Modern Art, the Corcoran Gallery in Washington, D.C., and the San Francisco Museum of Art, among others. His images have also been published in the *New Yorker, Vanity Fair, Double Take, Granta,* and other prominent magazines. Over the course of his career as a professional documentary photographer, he has had more than twenty solo exhibitions and has participated in numerous group shows. With Jerrilynn Dodds, Grazda spearheaded a project on the mosques of New York with a group of young Muslim architects, which led to an exhibit that included Grazda's images at the city's Storefront for Art and Architecture in the winter of 1996 and a book, *NY Masjid: The Mosques of New York,* with text by Jerrilynn Dodds (PowerHouse Books, 2002); the show also appeared in June 2009 at the Corcoran in Washington, D.C.

Grazda teaches photography at Harvard University and the International Center of Photography in New York. He has received grants from the New York Foundation for the Arts and the National Endowment for the Arts, and he has been a fellow at MacDowell Colony and the recipient of many awards.

Corniche, Muttrah, 2005

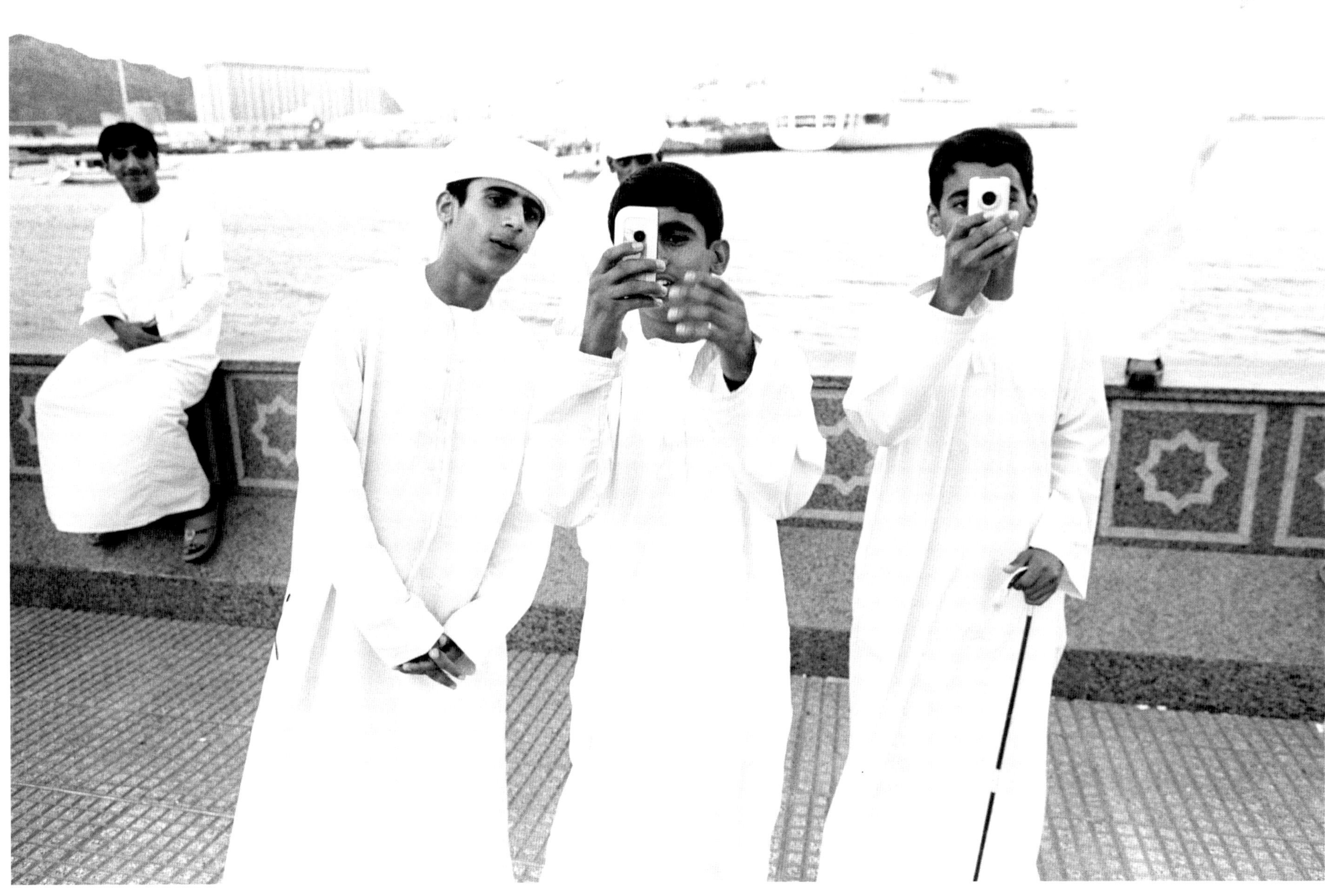

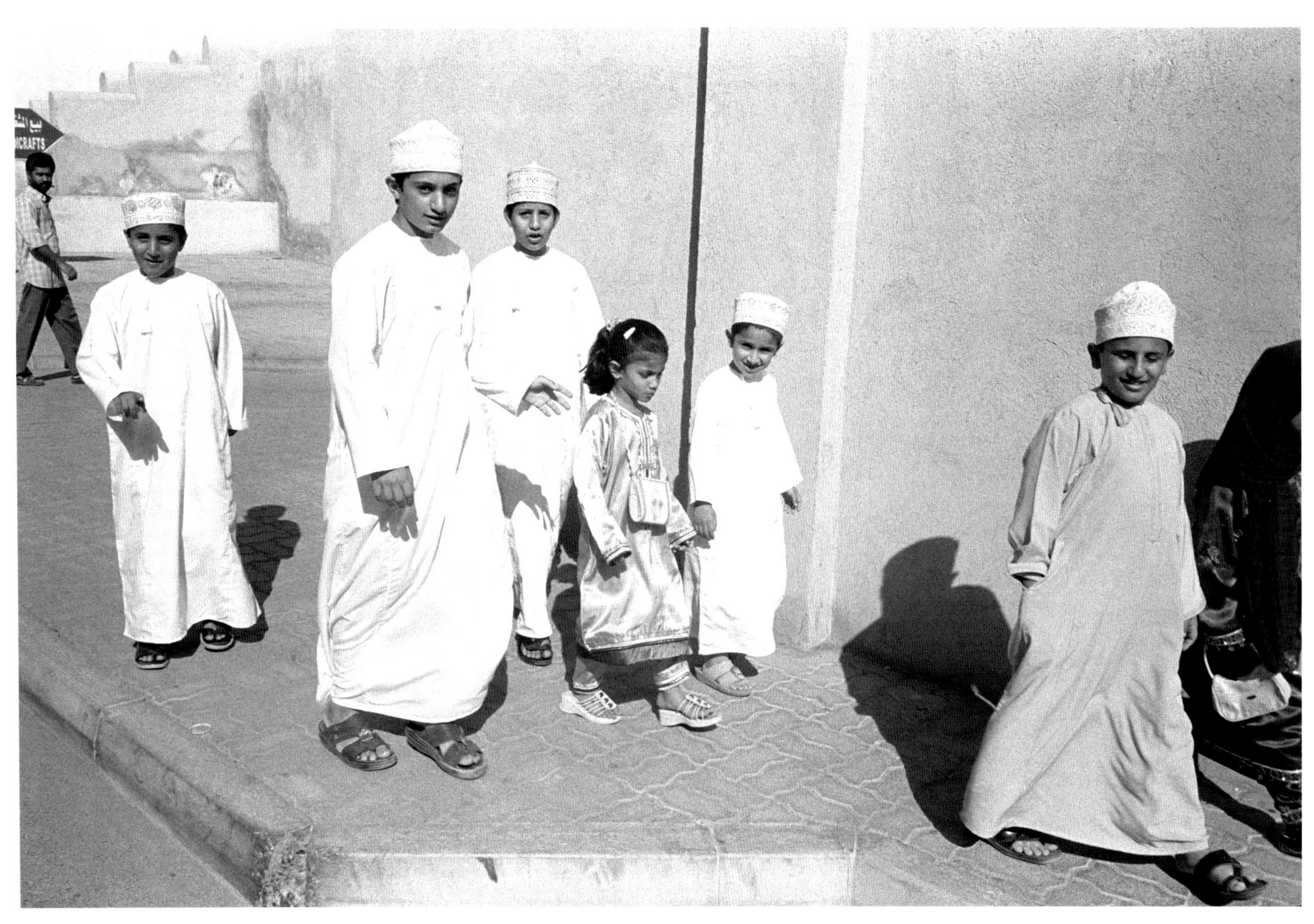

Children's Eid al-Fitr Market, Nizwa, 2005

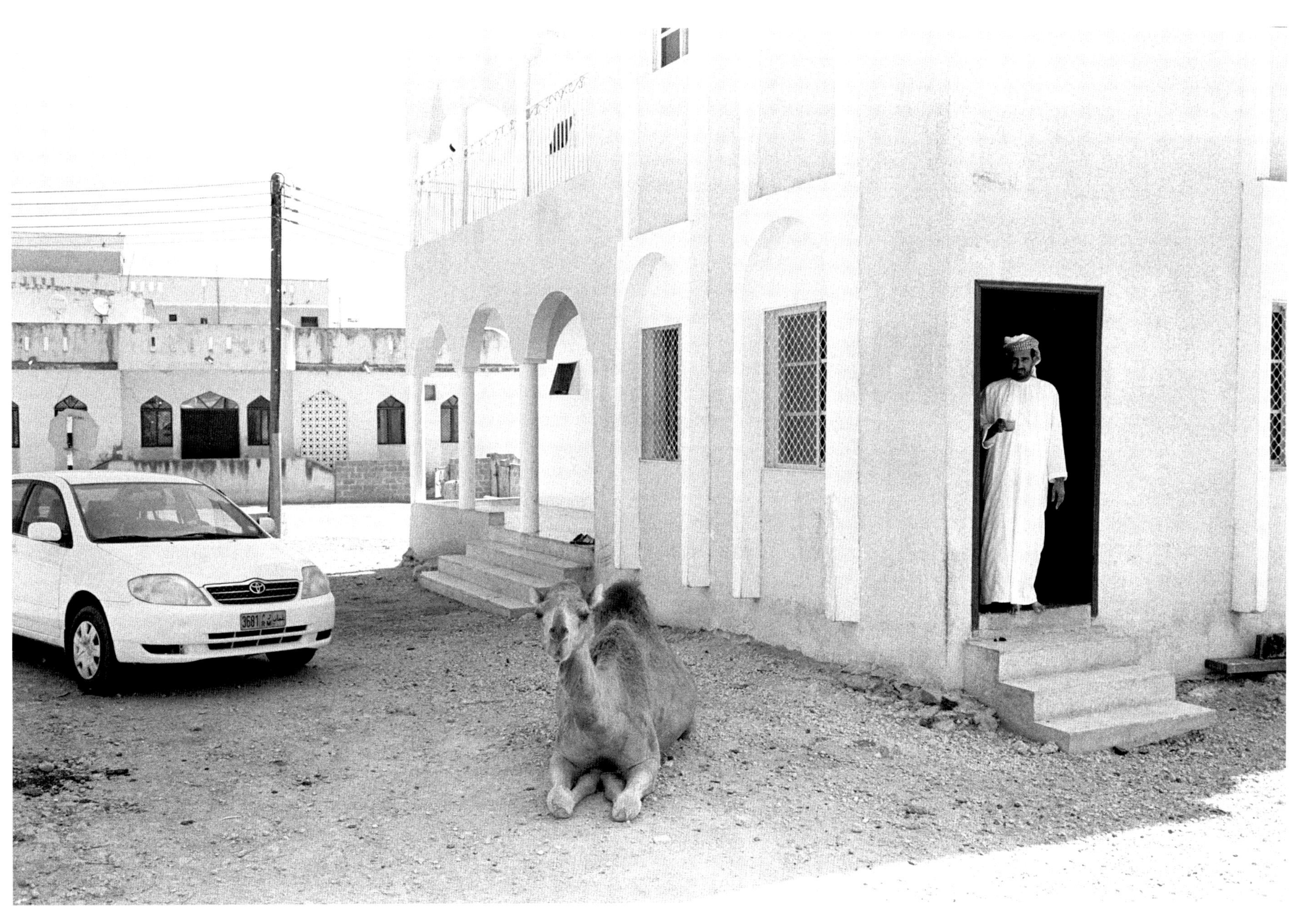

Dalkut, Dhofar, 2006

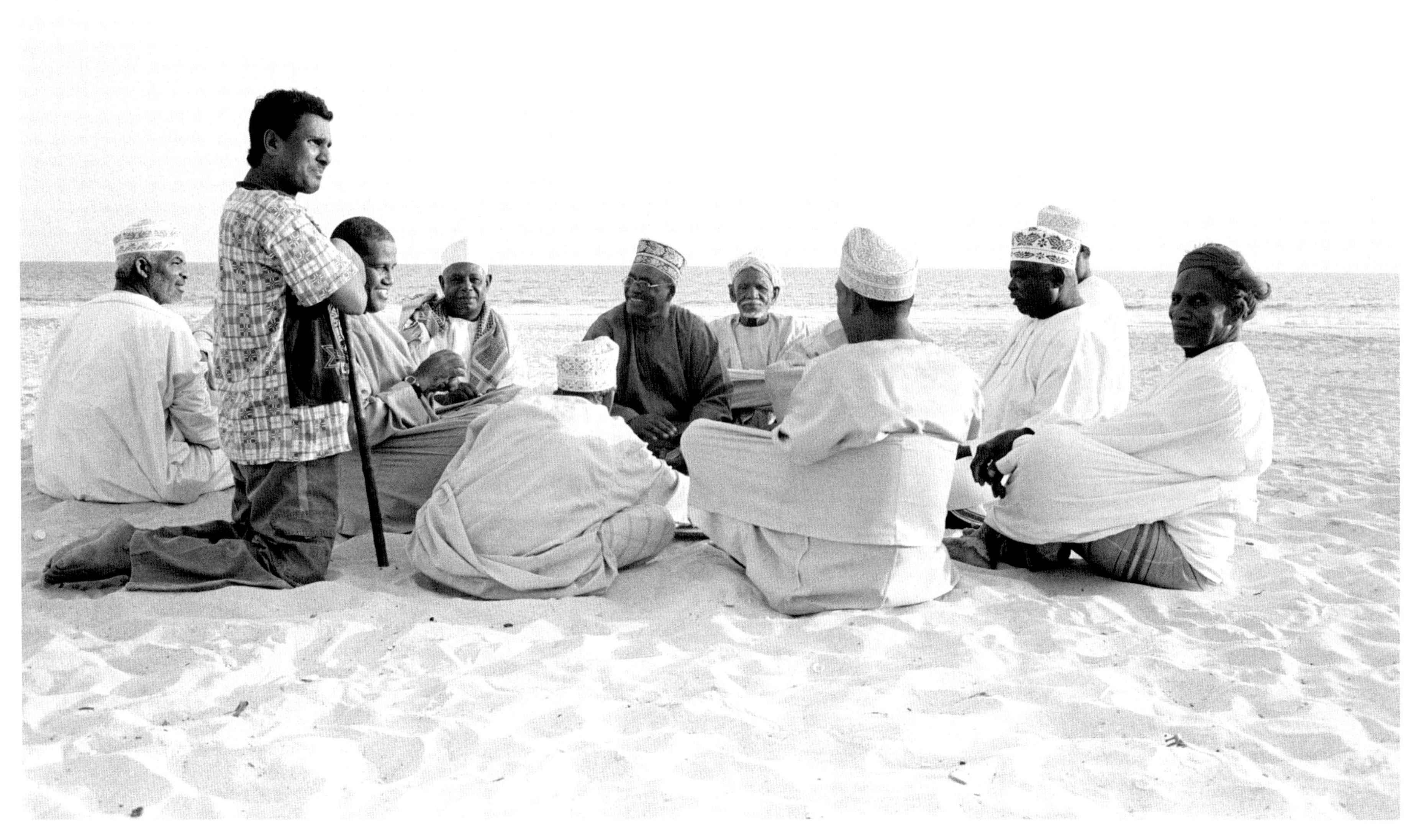

Salalah, Dhofar, 2006

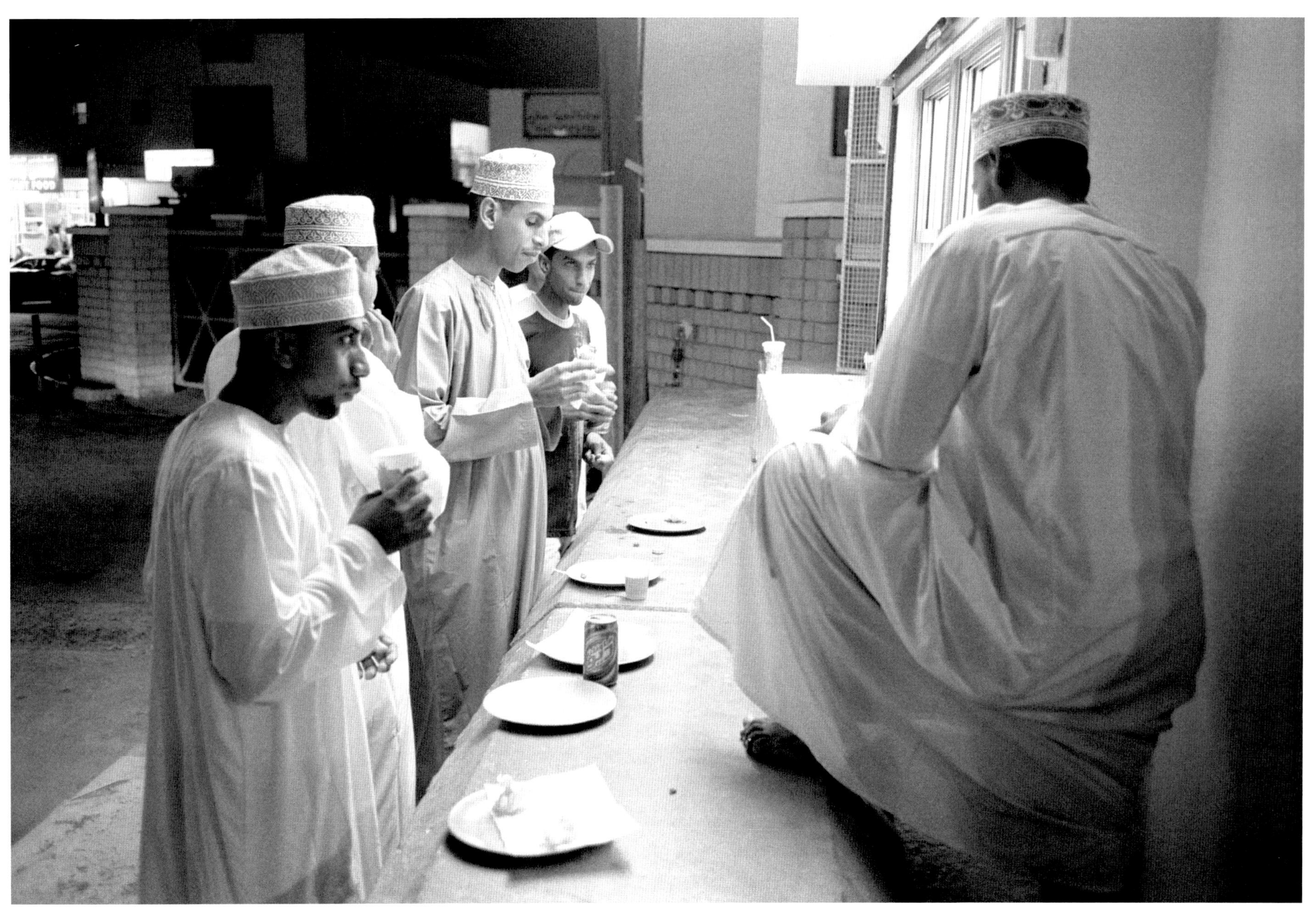

Corniche, Muttrah, 2006

Shopping mall, Ibri, 2005

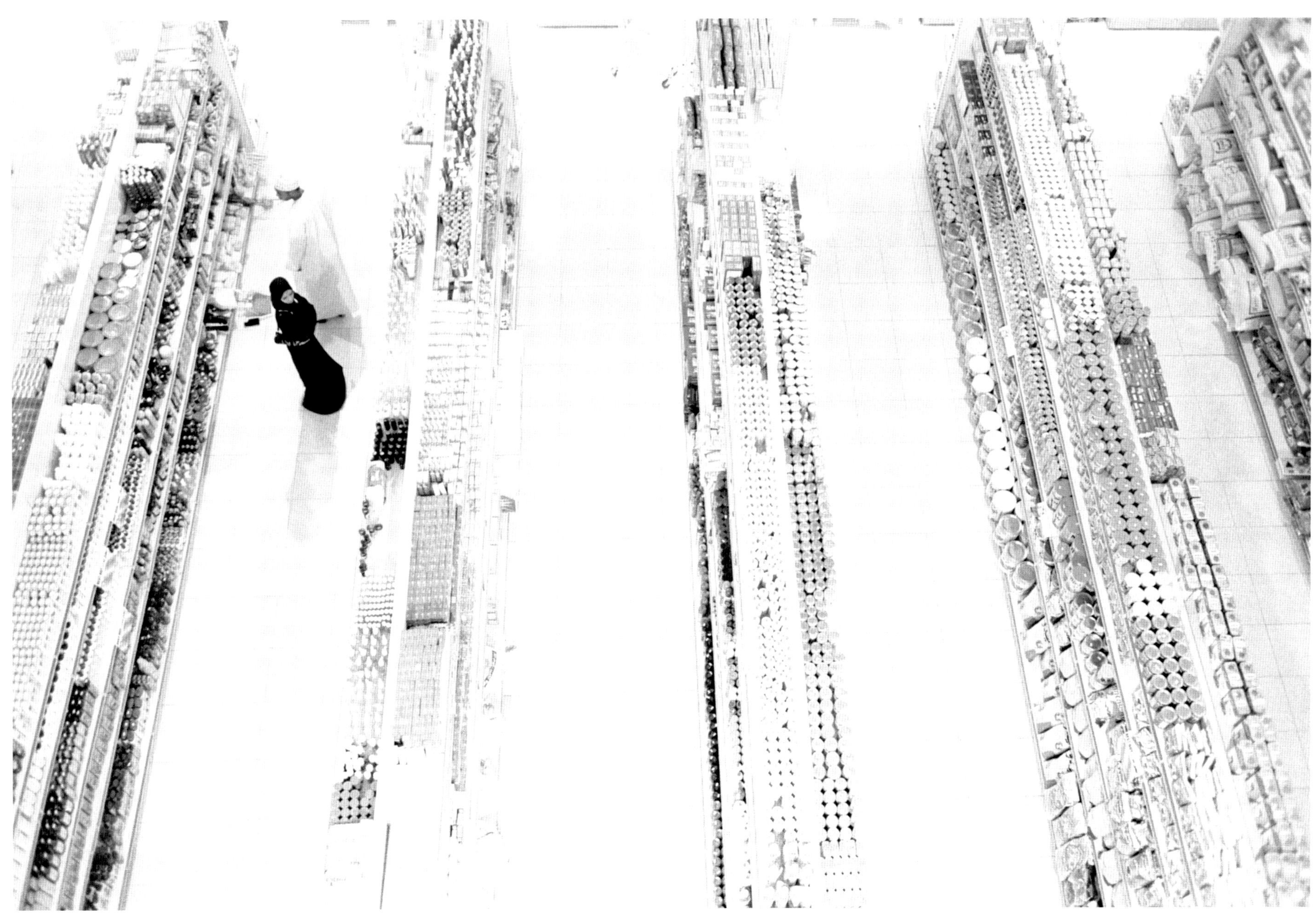

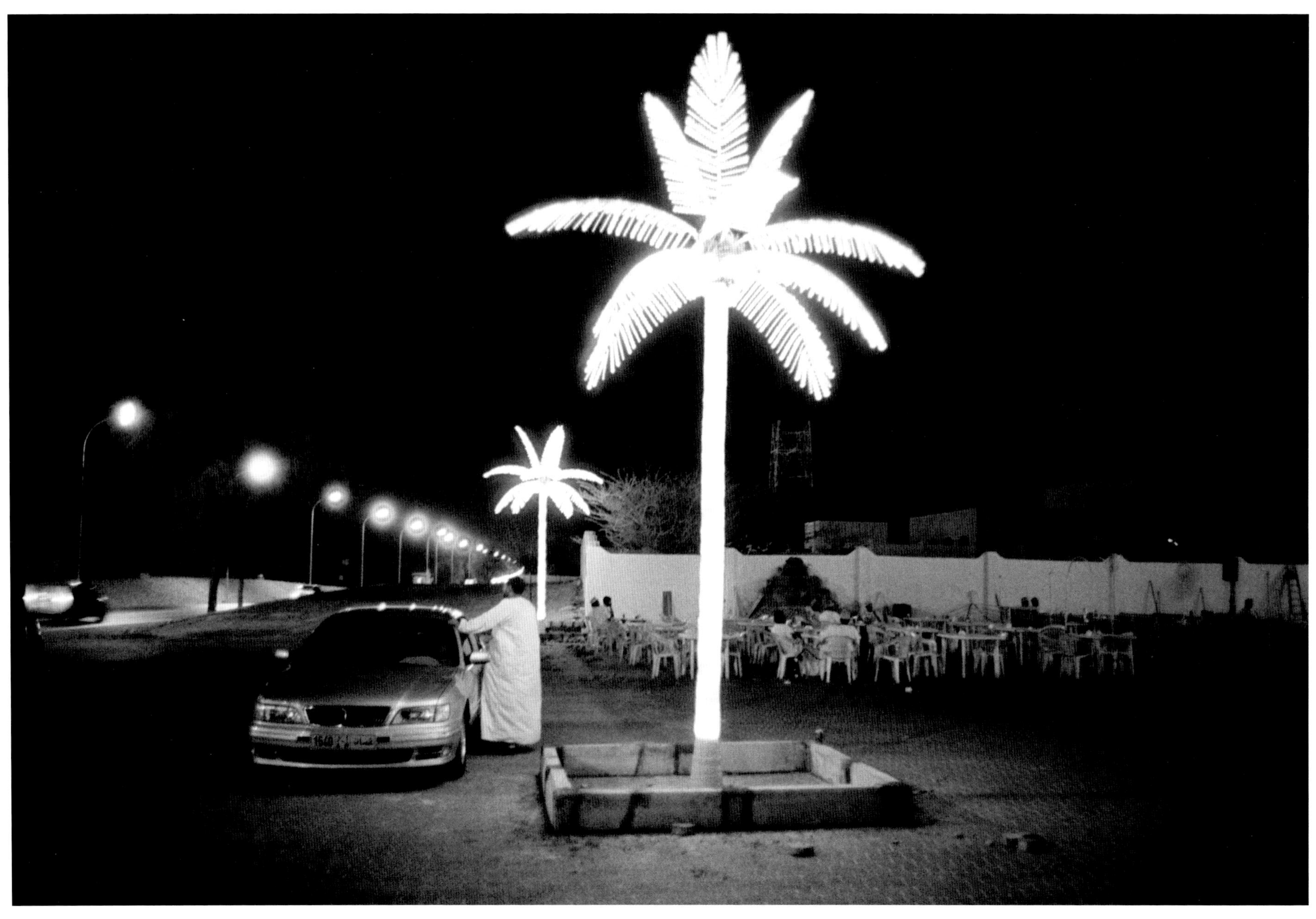

Nizwa, 2006

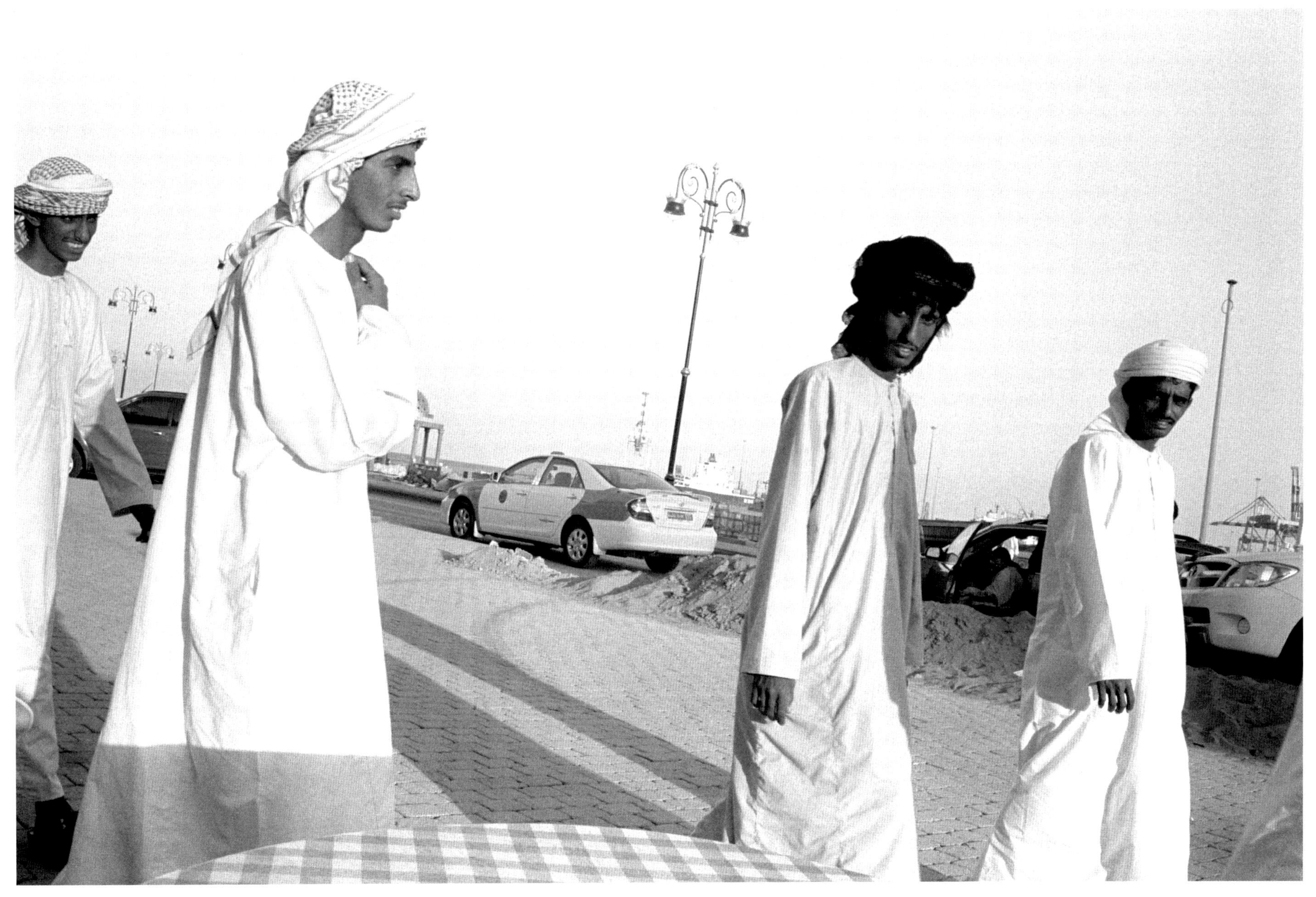

Corniche, Muttrah, 2005

CCC Shopping Center, Al Qurm, Muscat, 2006

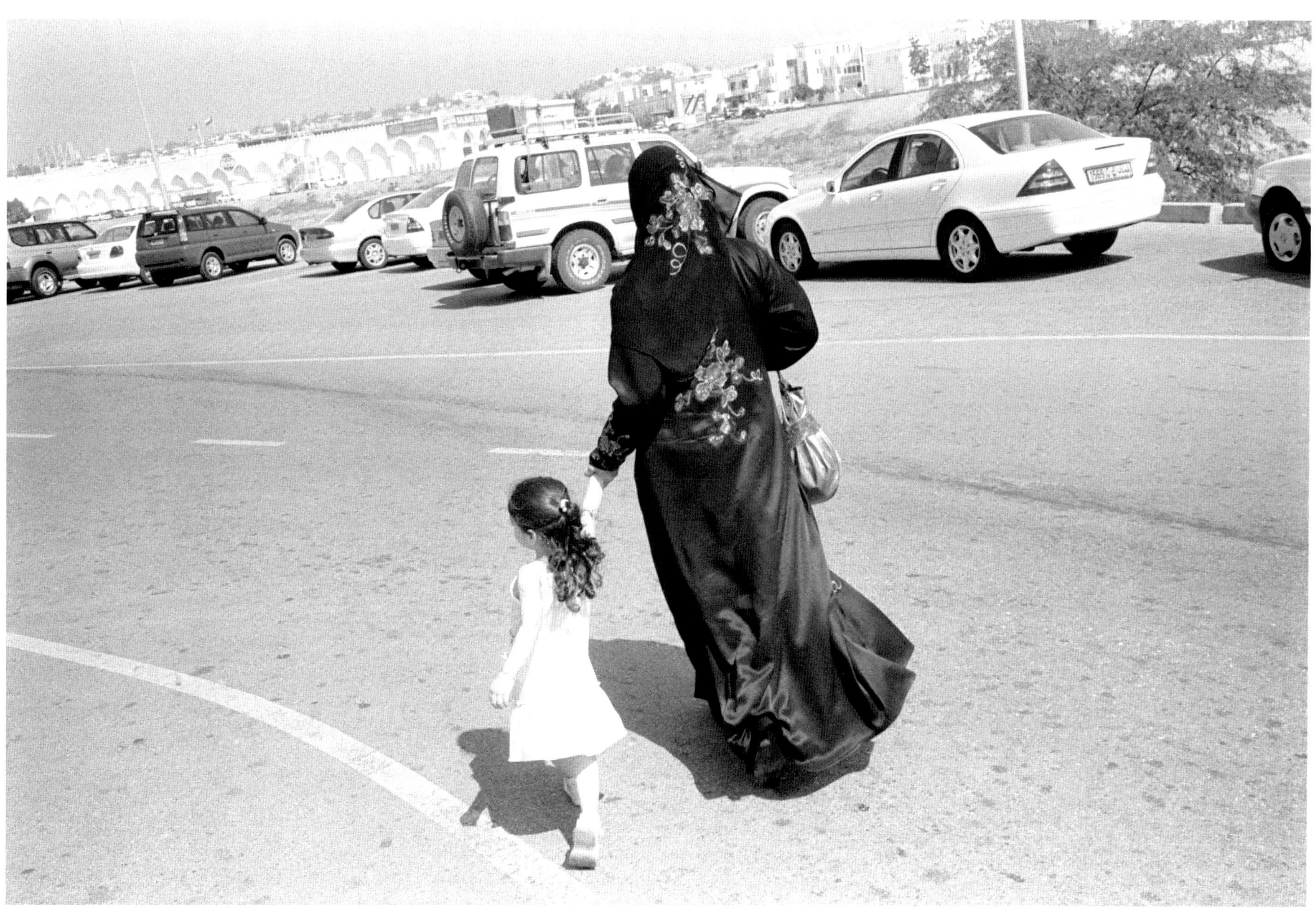

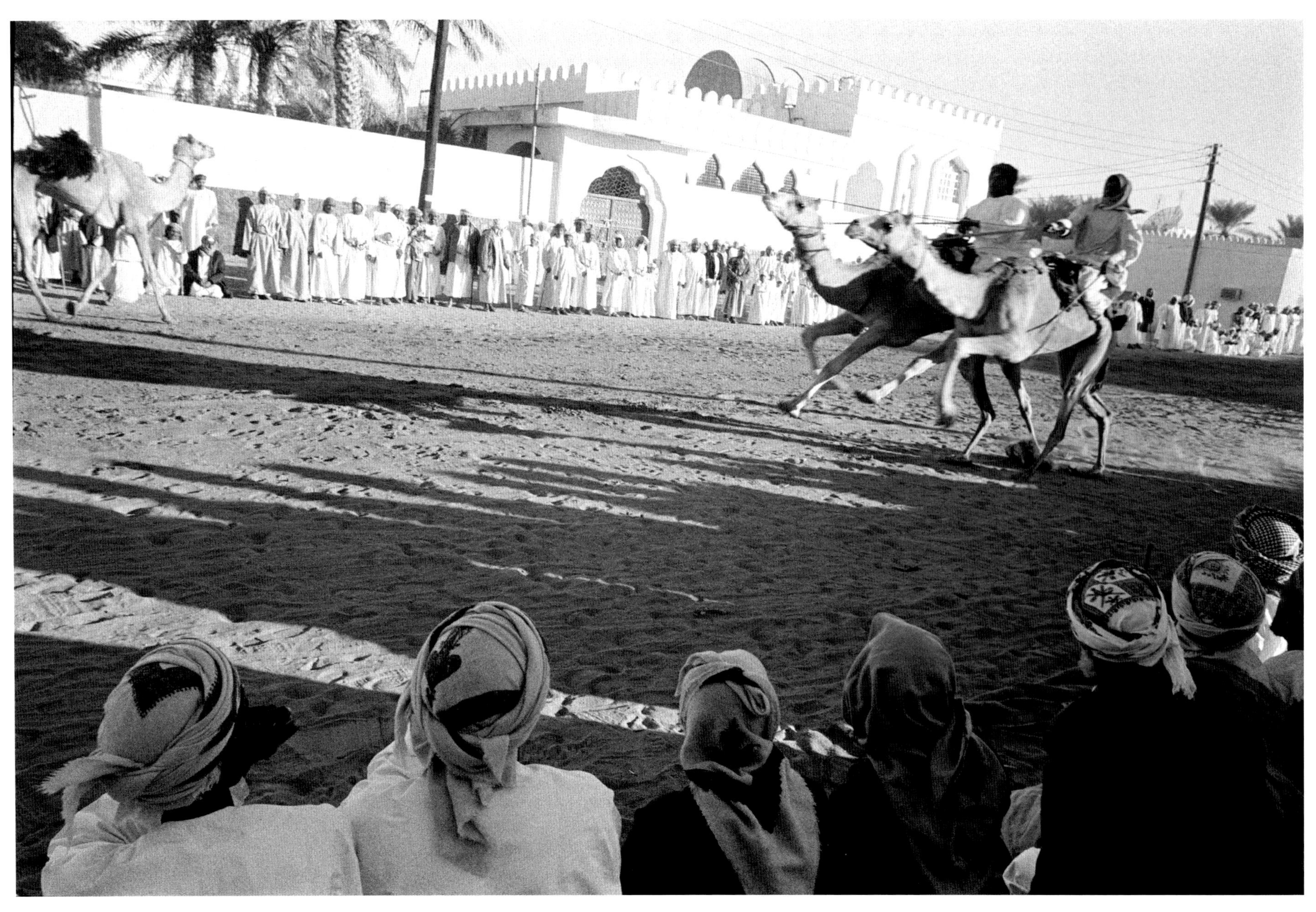

Eid al-Adha, Al-Mintatib, Bidiyah, 2006

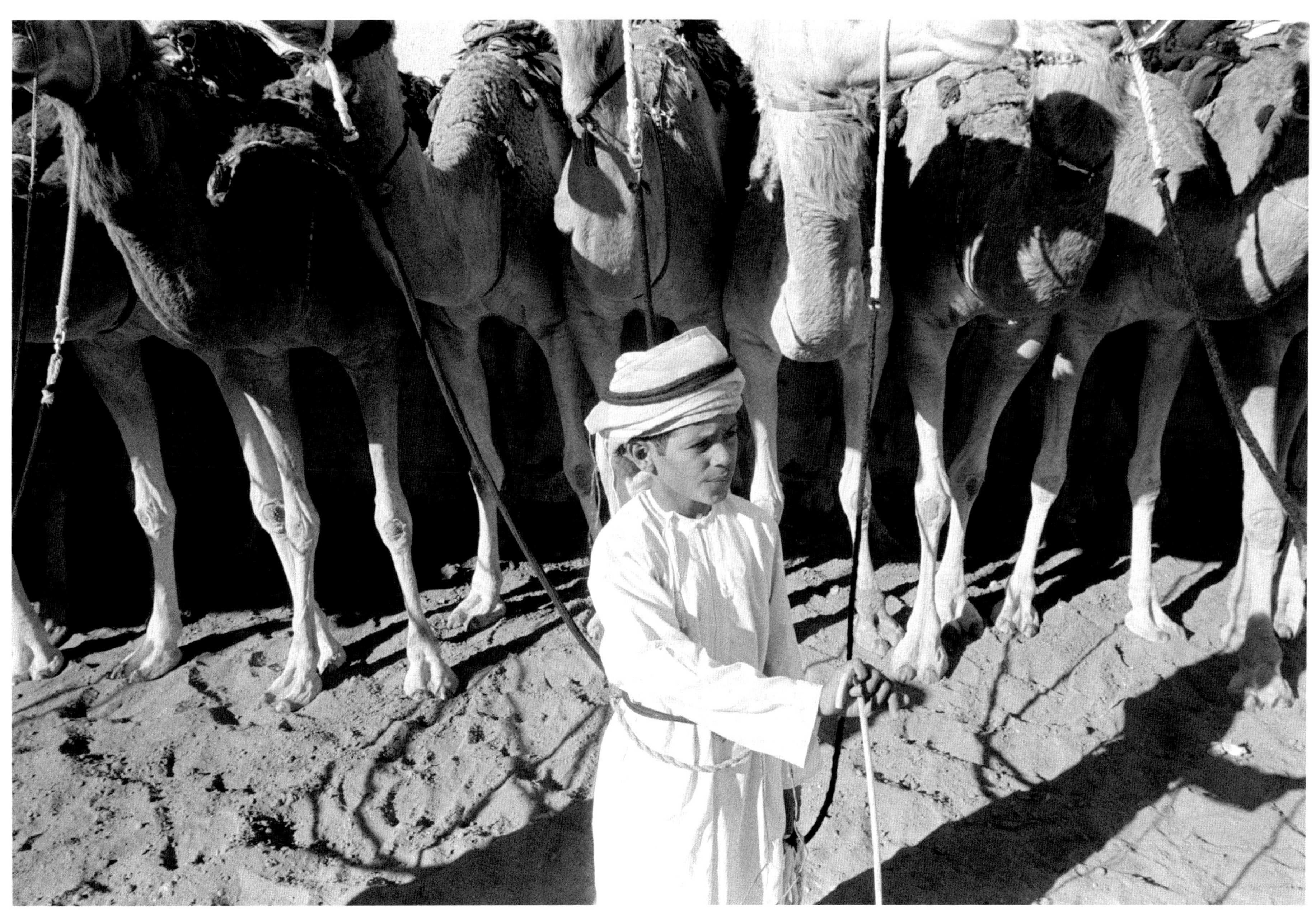

Eid al-Adha, Al-Mintatib, Bidiyah, 2006

Eid al-Adha, Al-Mintatib, Bidiyah, 2006

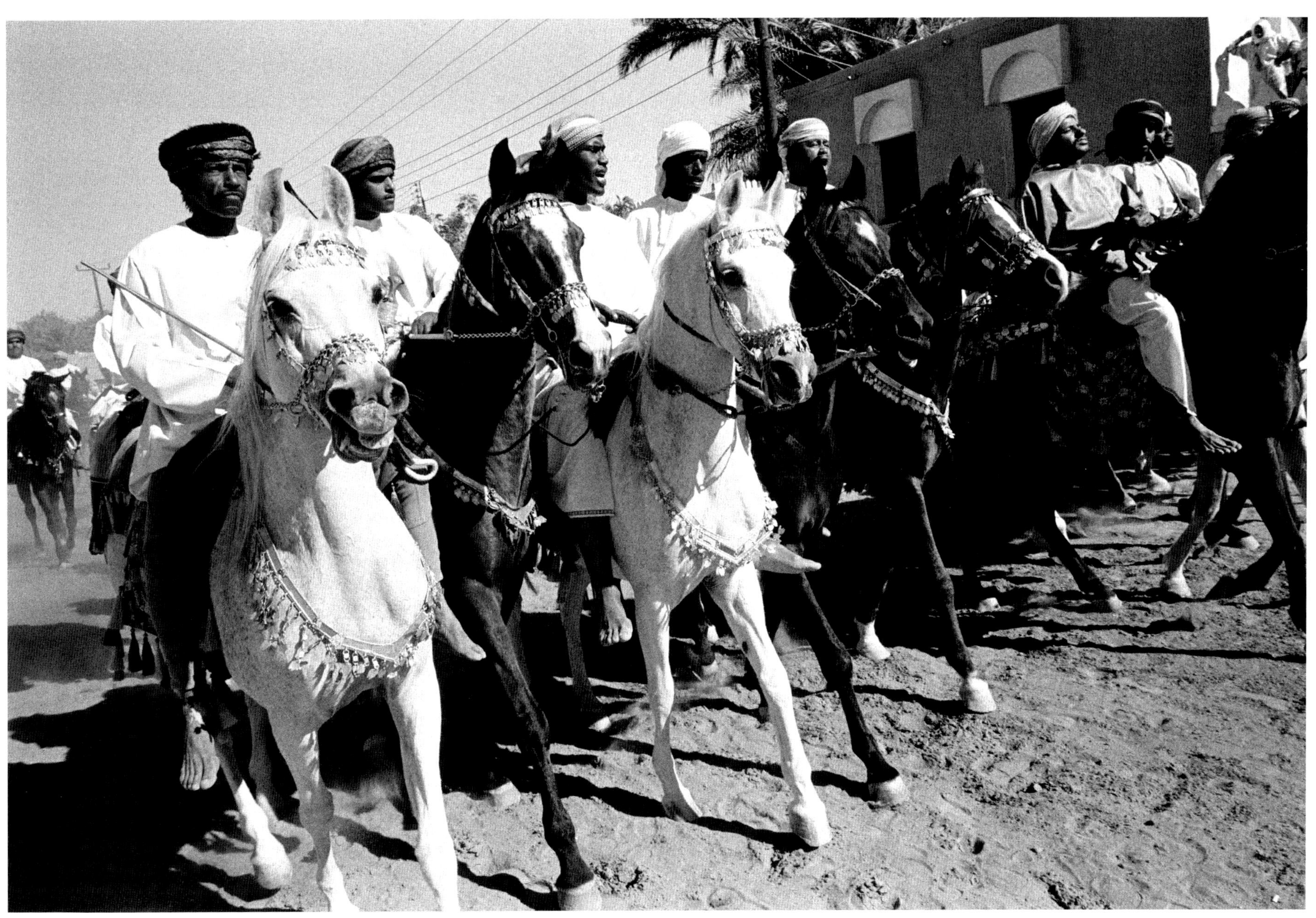

Wadi Bani Awf, 2006

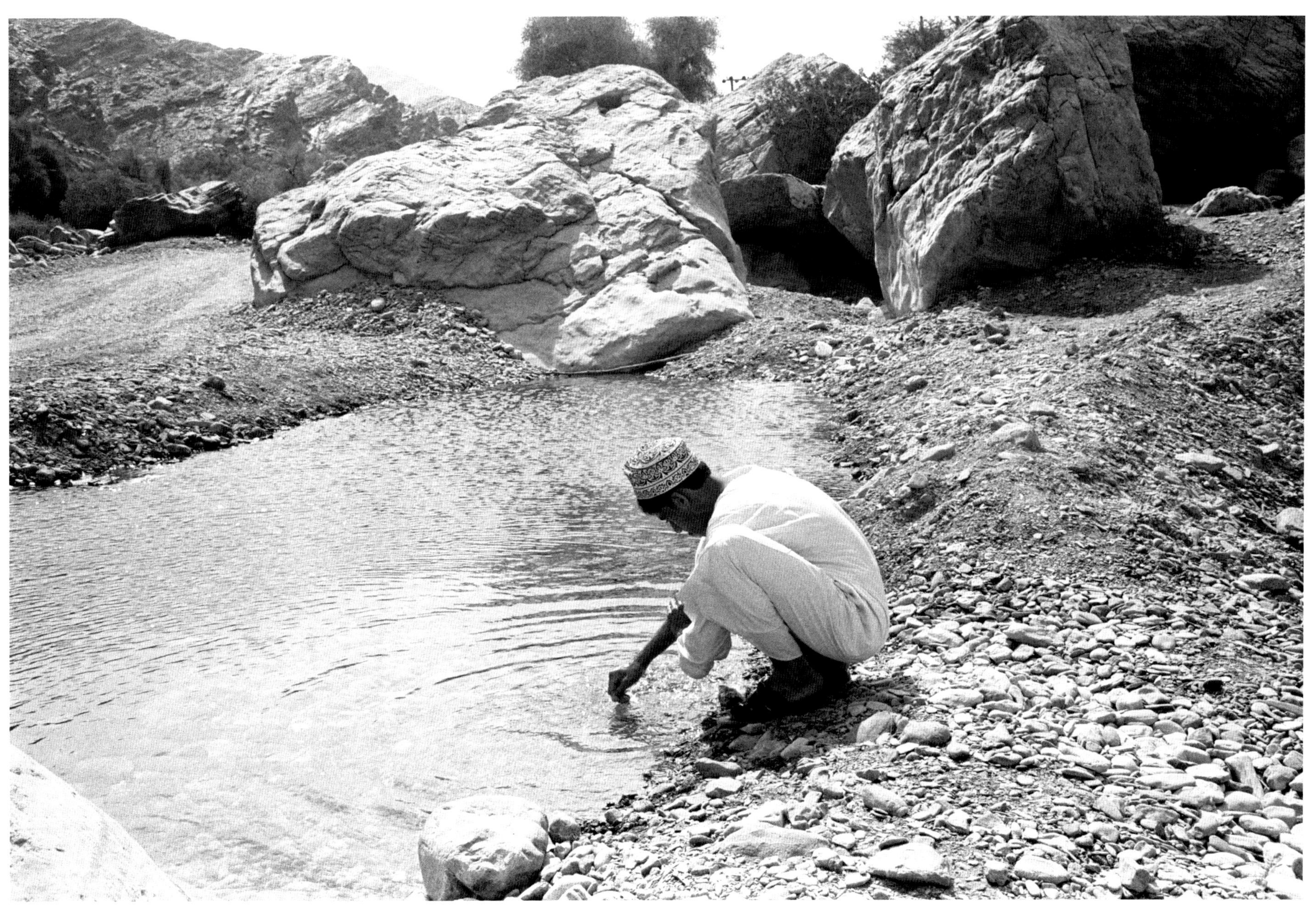

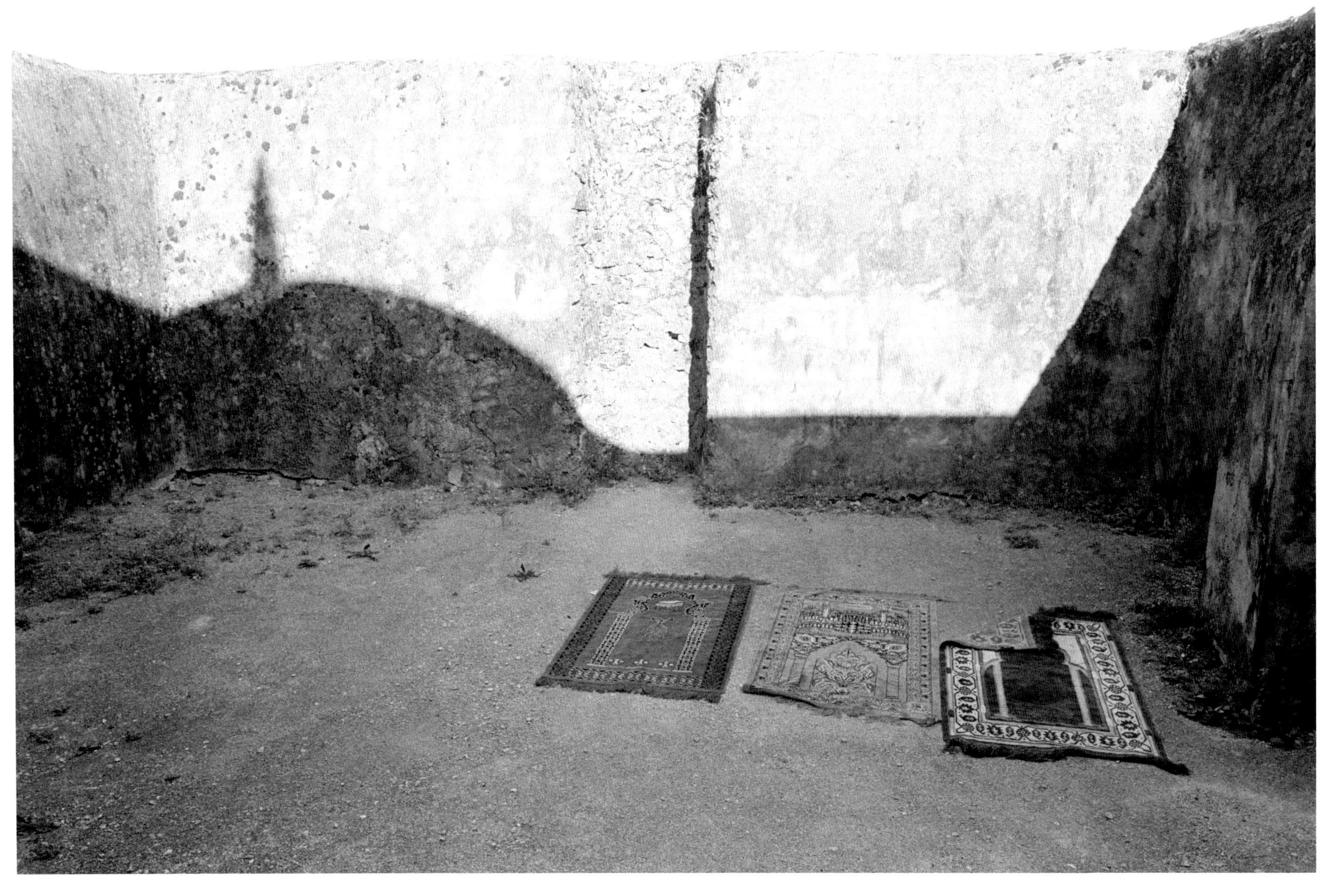

An Nabi Ayub (Job's Tomb), Atin, Dhofar, 2005

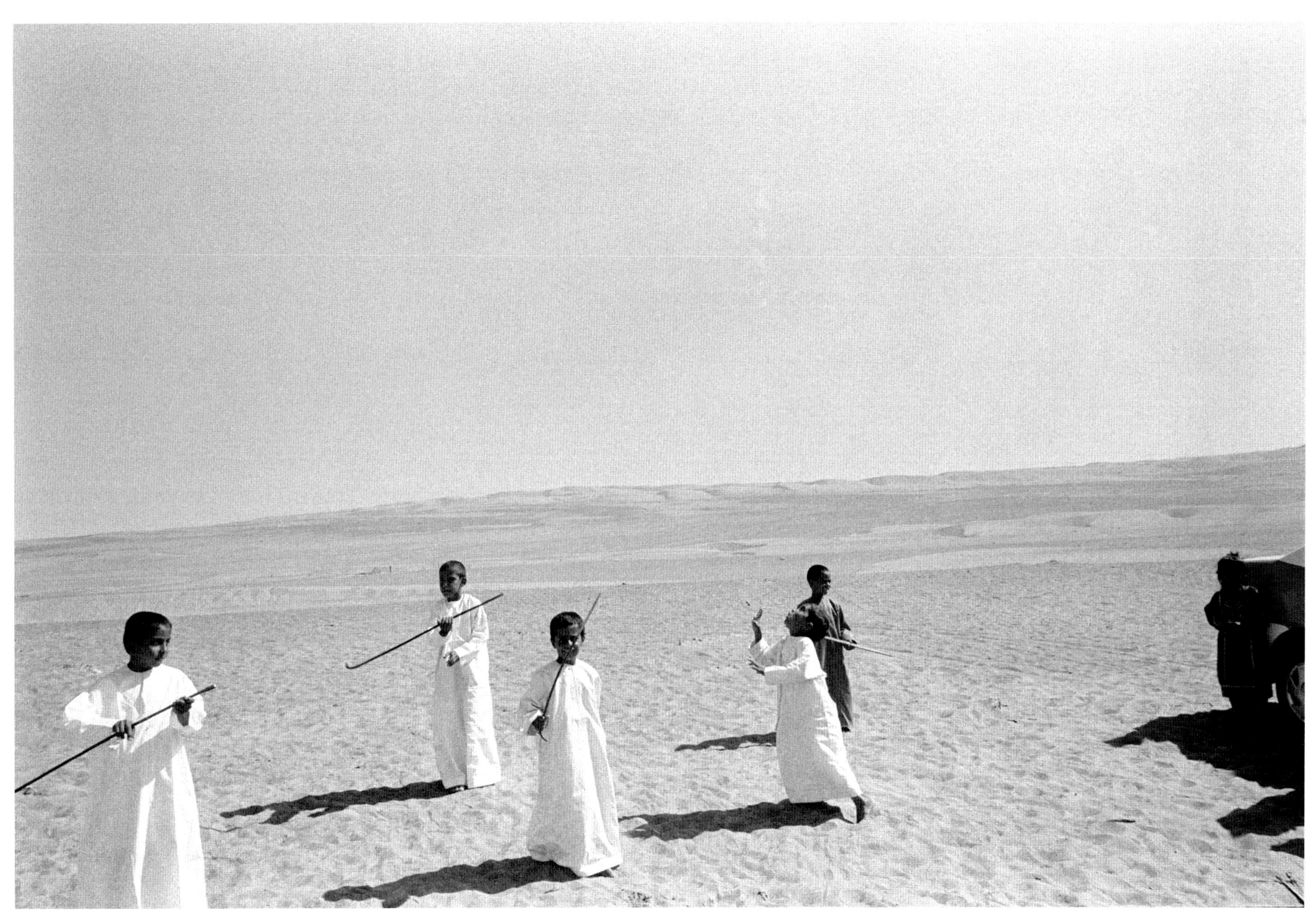

Eid, Bidiyah, 2006

Sur, 2006

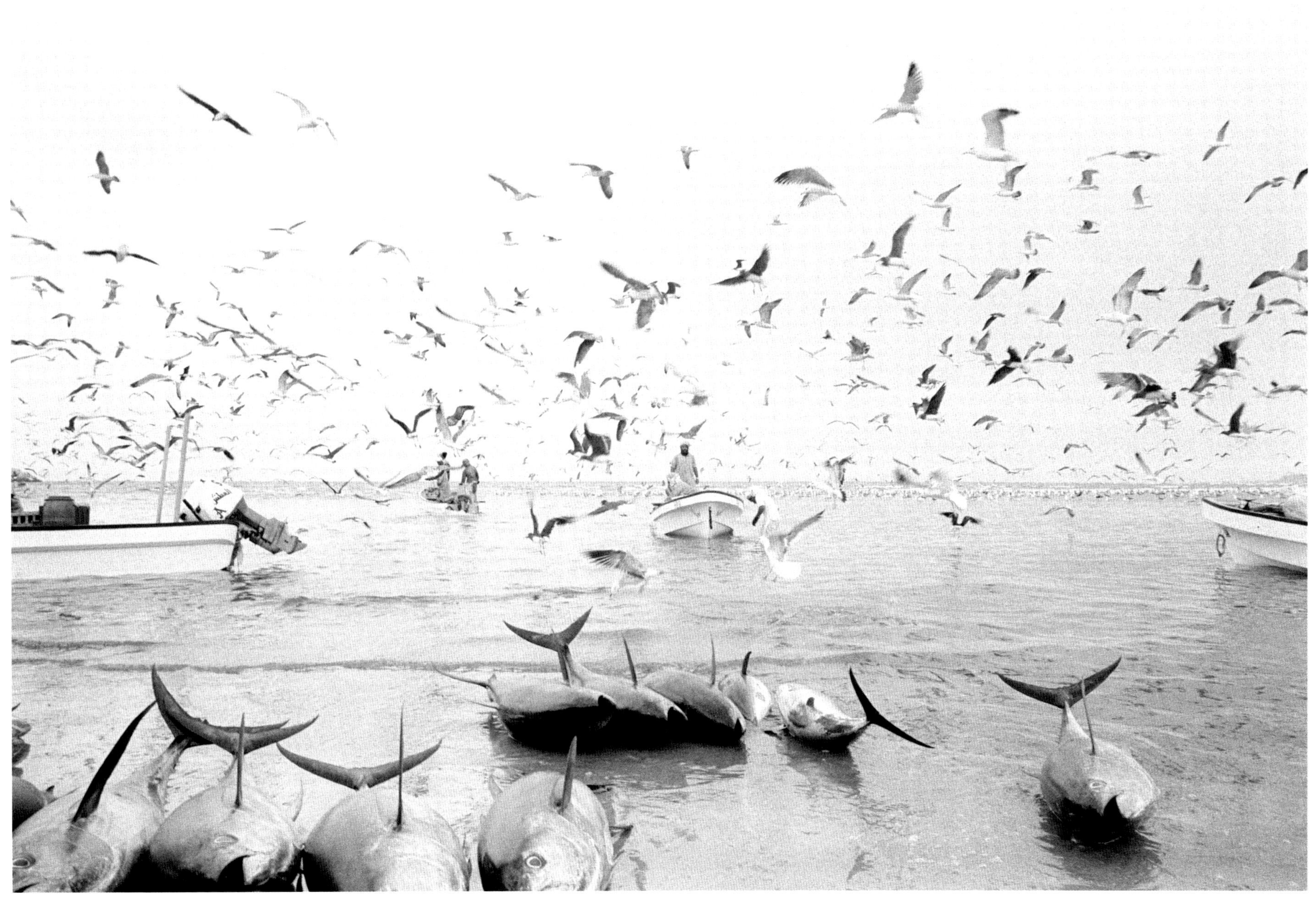

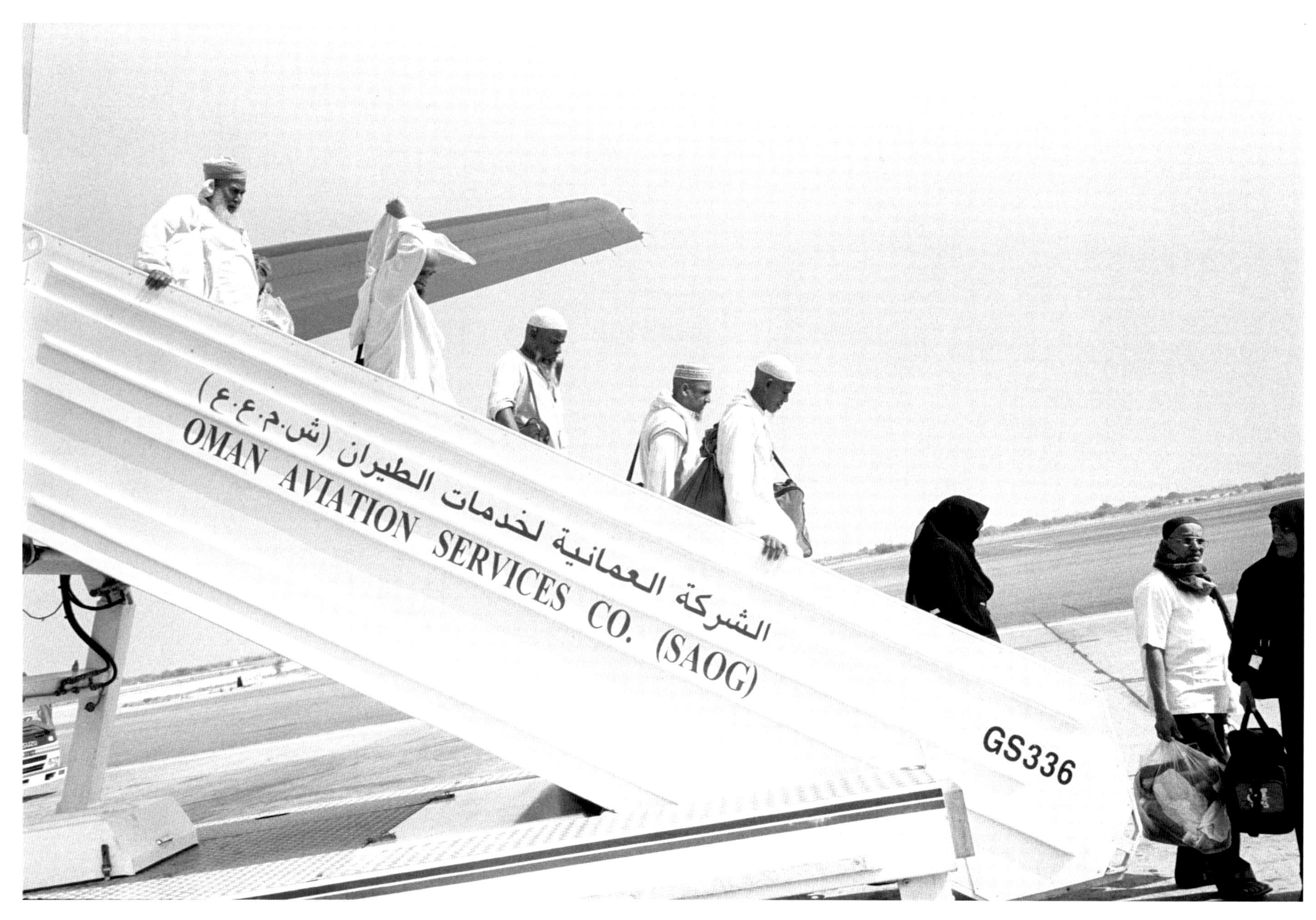

Returning from *haj*, As Sib Airport, 2006

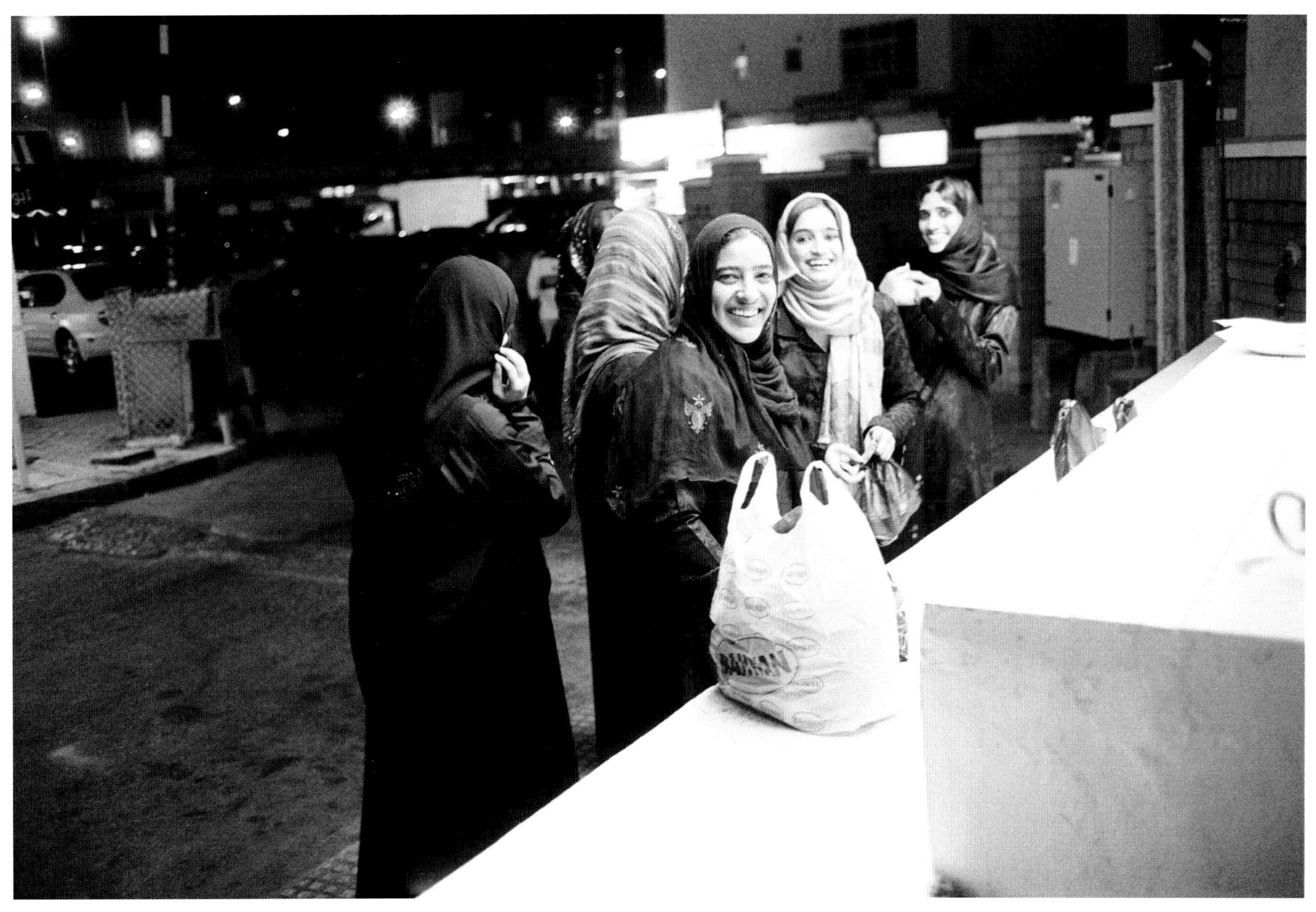

Corniche, Muttrah, 2006

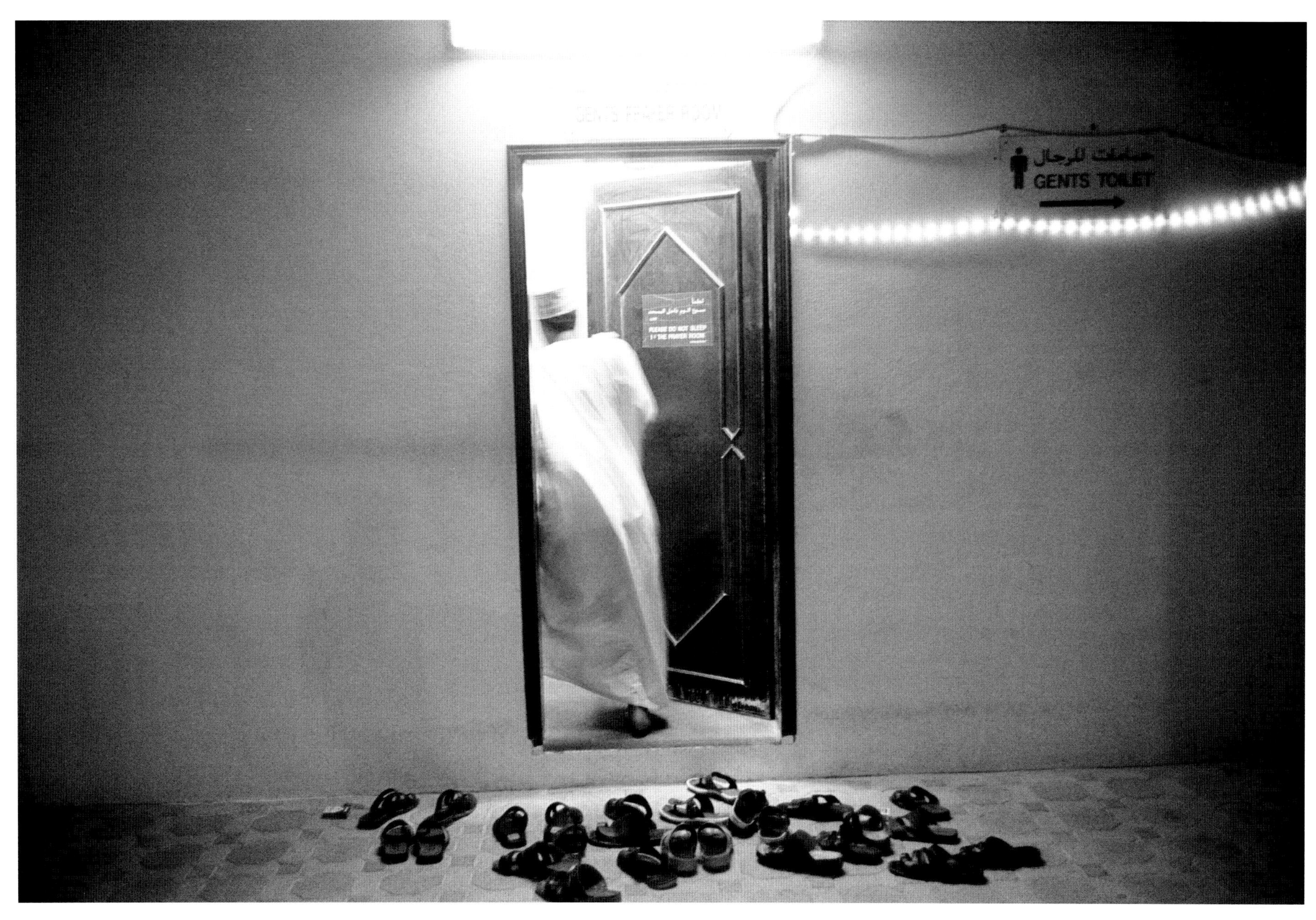

Al Ghaftain Rest House, Dhofar, 2006

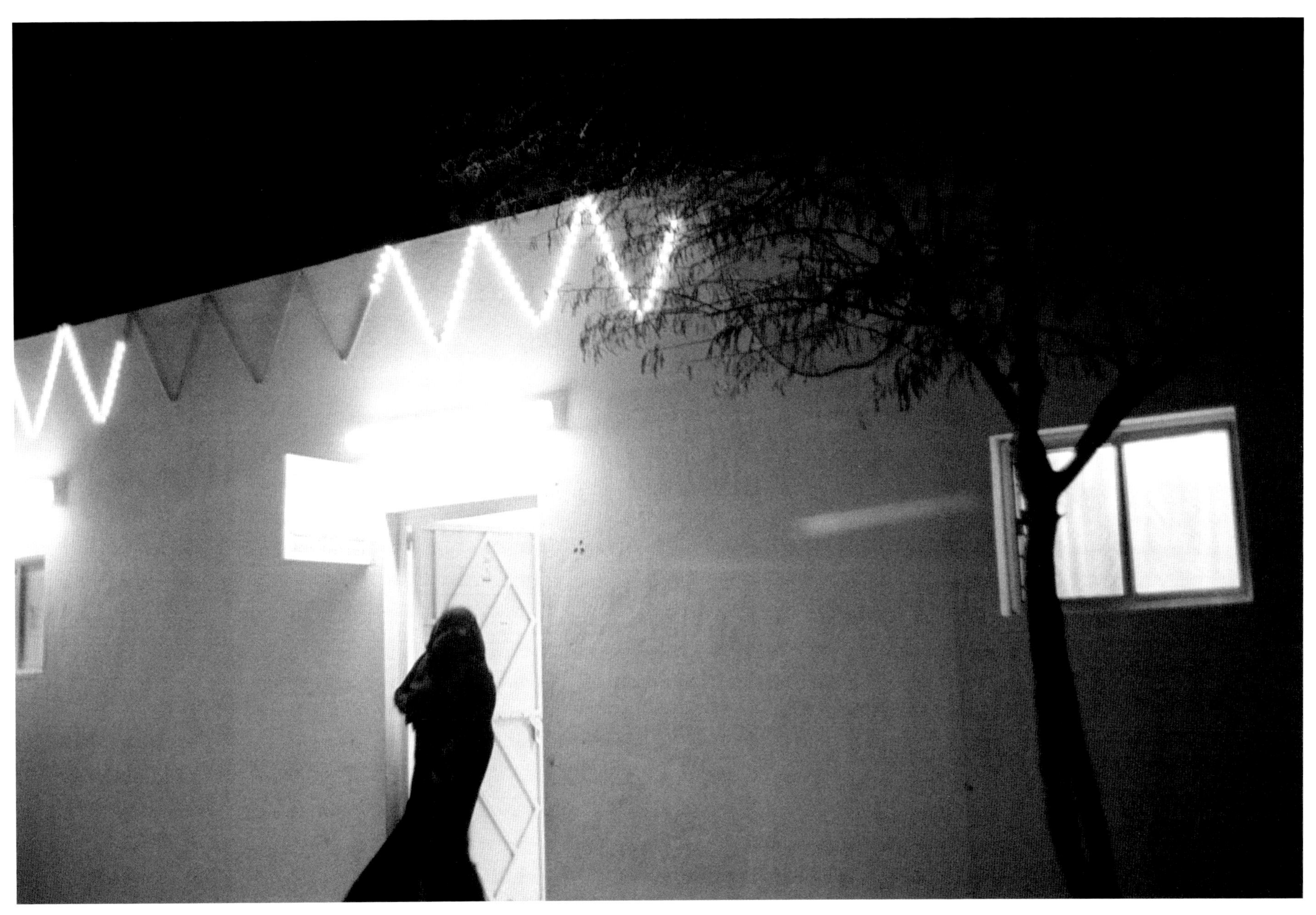

Al Ghaftain Rest House, 2006

Eid al-Adha, Al-Mintatib, Bidiyah, 2005

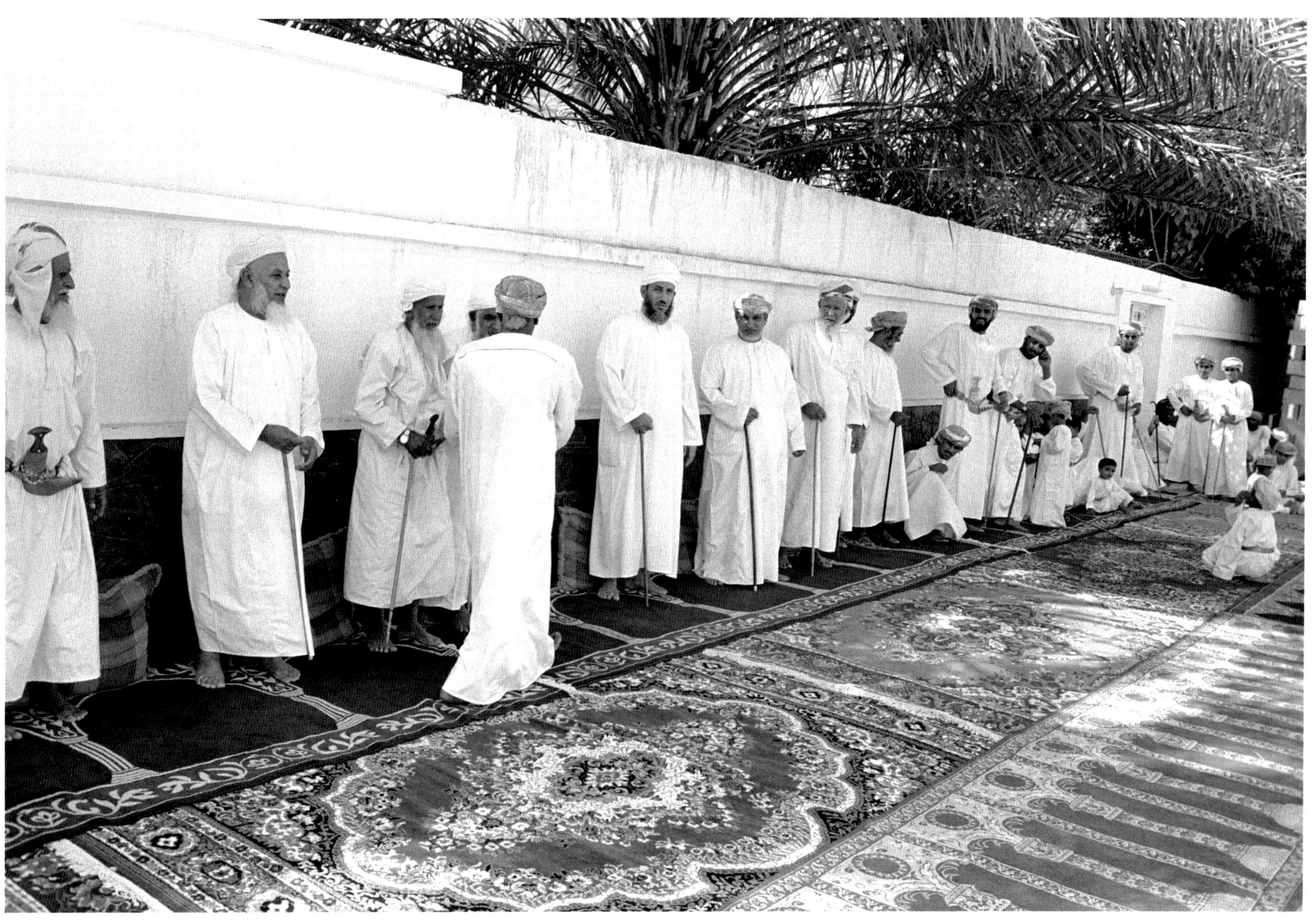

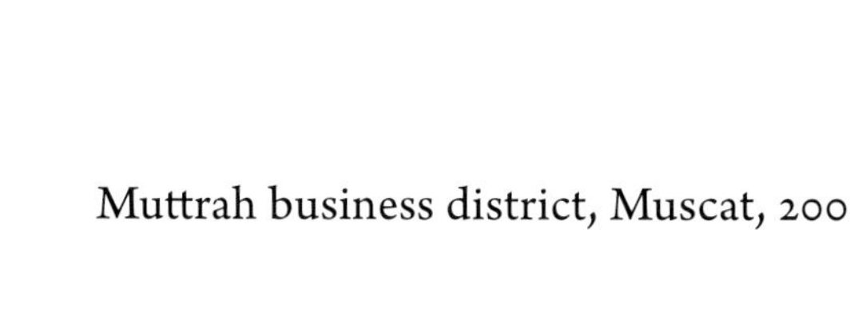

Muttrah business district, Muscat, 2006

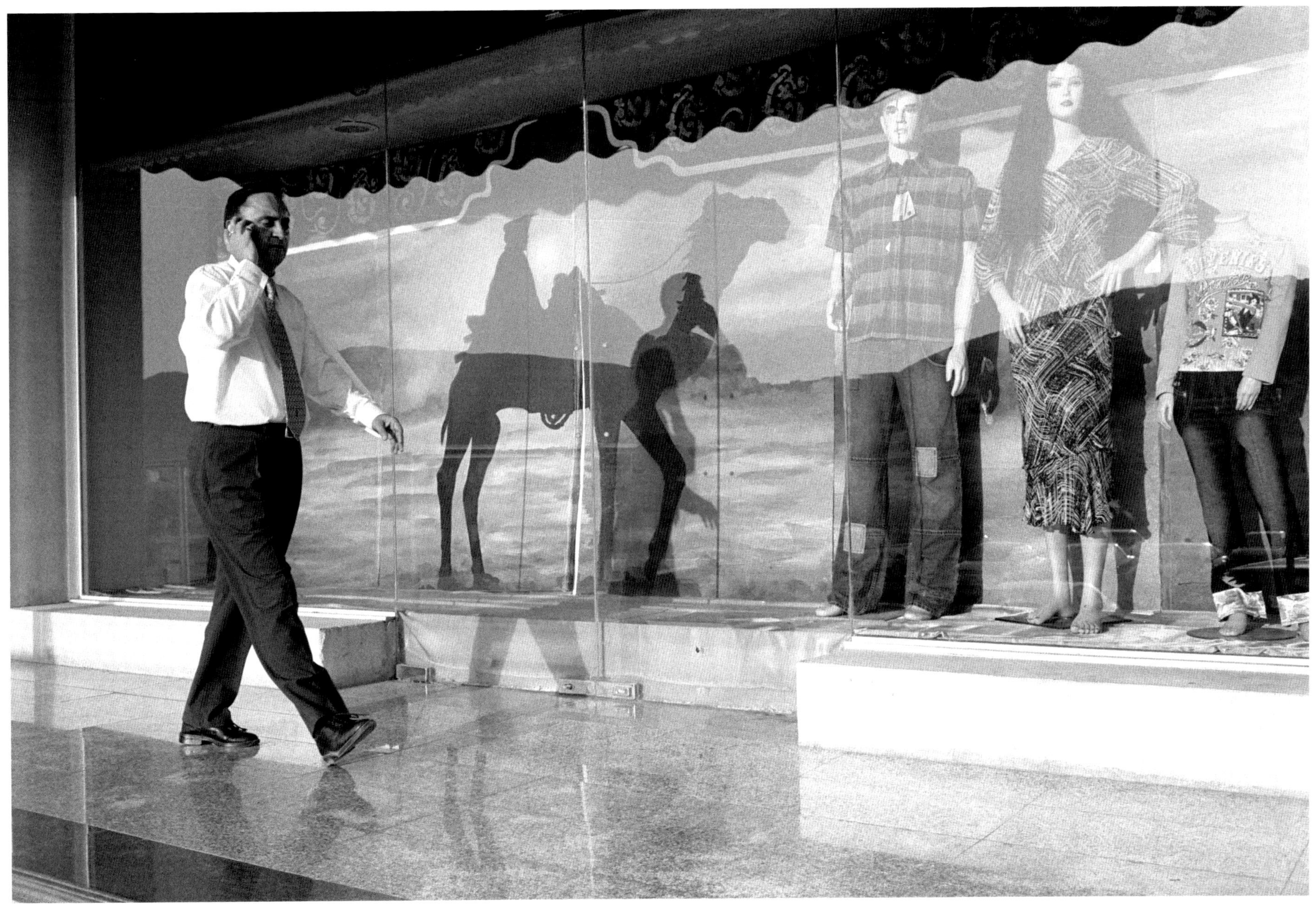

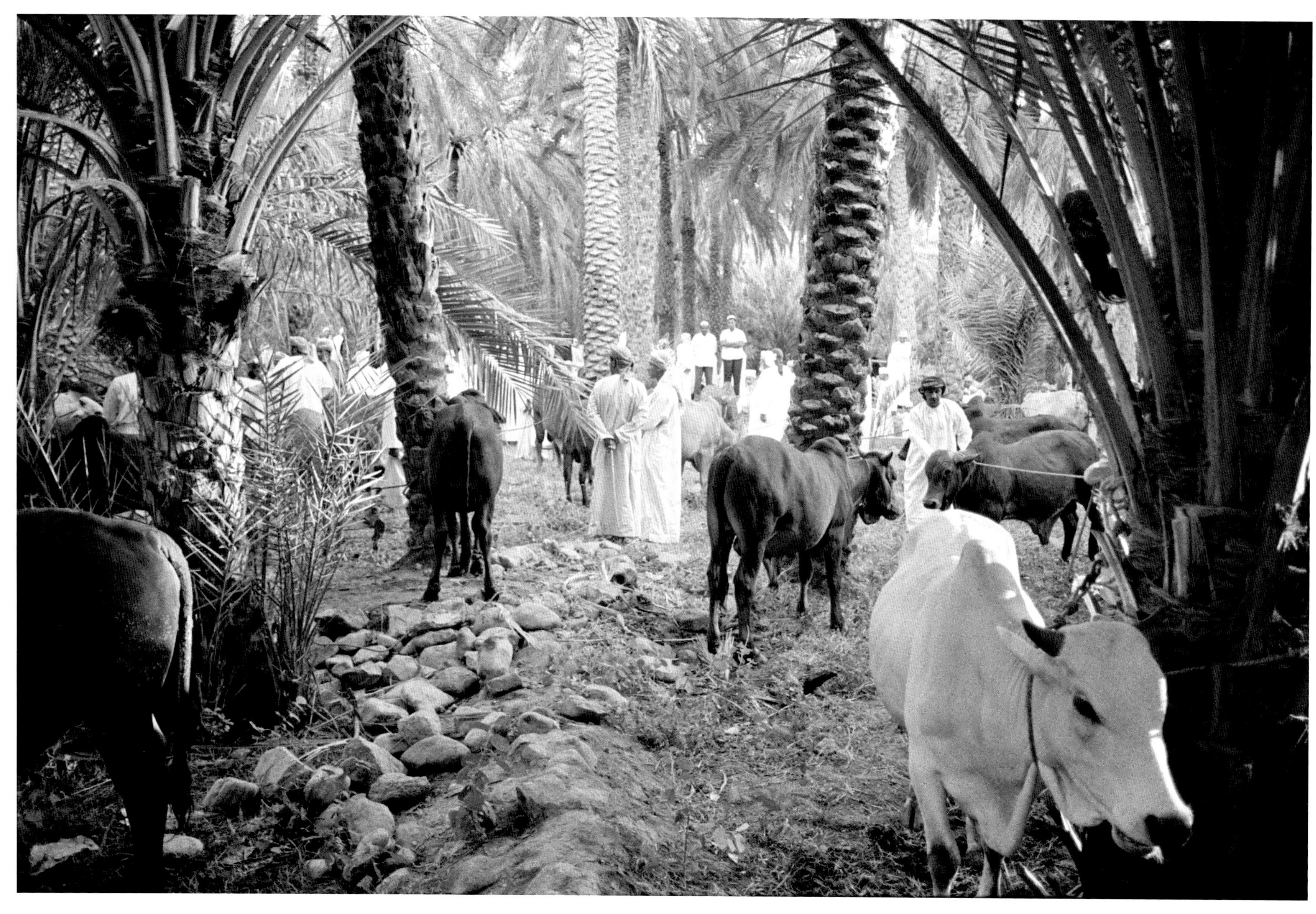

Eid market, Samail, 2005

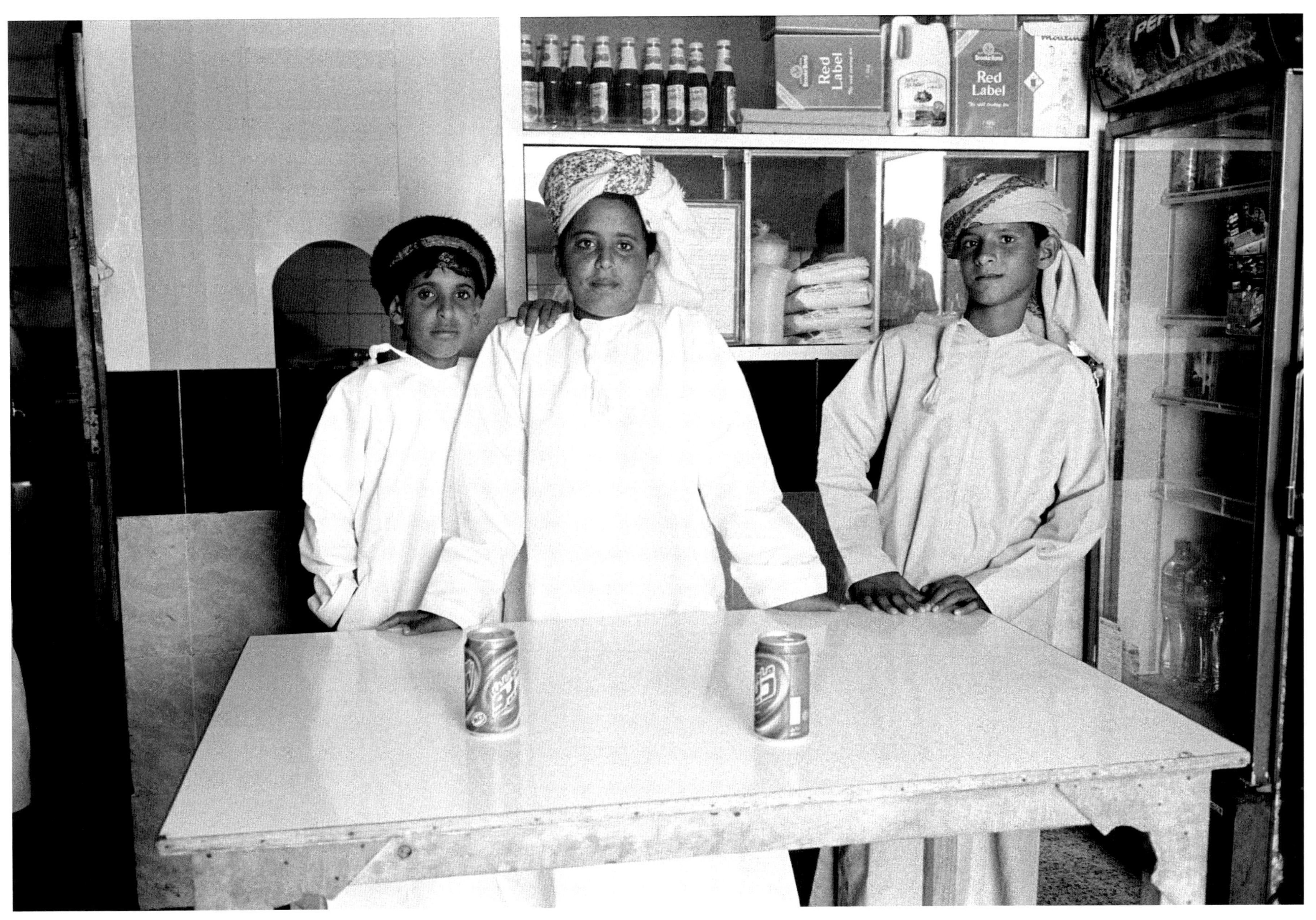

As Siwayh, 2006

Notes

This book is a joint publication of

Broadway Publications,
an imprint of the Institute
for American Values

1841 Broadway, Suite 211
New York, NY 10023
www.americanvalues.org

AND

The Ministry of Awqaf
and Religious Affairs

P.O. Box 3232
Ruwi 112
Oman